THE LITTLE BOOK OF

FAST BIKES

Written by Jon Stroud

THE LITTLE BOOK OF
FAST BIKES

This edition first published in the UK in 2007
By Green Umbrella

© Green Umbrella Publishing 2007

www.greenumbrella.co.uk

Publishers Jules Gammond & Vanessa Gardner

Printed and bound in China

ISBN-13: 978-1-905828-25-8

Contents

Aprilia RS250
1995 Italy

FANCY A MOTOGP BIKE BUT CAN'T quite stretch to the budget of Valentino Rossi's YZR? With its howling two-stroke power plant, sublime handling and bodywork directly copied from the factory racers, the Aprilia RS250 is about as close to a GP bike as reasonable money can buy.

Originally introduced in 1995 and then revised for 1998, the Italian pocket-rocket was hailed a classic of its time and revered for its stunning Latino looks and pin-point handling. It is testament to the skill of the RS250's designers that now, even more than a decade on, it looks as fresh as ever and is still a popular second-hand choice for the discerning road rider or track-day junkie.

Powered by a Suzuki six-speed, two-stroke 249cc v-twin (originally found strapped to the all conquering RGV250) married to Aprilia's own exhaust system, the RS produces almost 65bhp and 40Nm of torque. This may not sound much compared to the 170+ bhp produced by the big 1000cc superbikes of today but when you realise that this equates to an astonishing 258bhp per litre on a machine that weighs in at a sylphlike 140kg, it becomes apparent that this bambino replica racer is something special indeed. Lower through the rev range it does have a tendency to struggle a little, however, as soon as you hit

the magic 8,000rpm mark it explodes into life, taking on the characteristics of a guided missile with a soundtrack to match.

SPECIFICATION

Capacity: 249cc
Type: 2-Stroke 90° V-twin
Bore: 56mm
Stroke: 50.6mm
Compression Ratio: 13.2:1
Dry Weight: 140kg
Maximum Power: 64.3bhp @ 10,400rpm
Maximum Torque: 40Nm @ 10,750rpm
Maximum Speed: 130mph

Unusually for a 250cc machine, the riding position is far from cramped with its twin-spar polished magnesium alloy frame, Showa upside-down forks and low swept clip-on bars complementing the package perfectly and adding further to the GP racer feel.

However, thanks to the tightening of European emissions laws the production of a cost-effective, high-performance two-stroke machine became impossible. With the Aprilia RS250's days sadly numbered, production was ceased in 2003 but many fine examples still exist on both the road and the racetrack.

Aprilia RSV1000SP
1999 Italy

CONSIDERING HOW LONG IT CAN take some bike manufacturers to get things right, the RSV Mille is an astonishing achievement. When initially introduced in 1998 the Italian manufacturer had built its reputation almost exclusively on wailing two-stroke race replicas and knobbly-tyred trail bikes but, in an instant, that all changed. Here was Aprilia's first ever large capacity sportsbike and it was a gem. Powerful, poised and exceptionally good looking, this was a machine that was fast enough to take on the might of Japan and exclusive enough to compete on a level playing field with Bologna's best known two-wheeled export – Ducati.

From the outset, everything about the Mille was new and different. The canvas for this creation was a sculpted cast alloy twin-spar frame that drew heavily from experience gained through their factory GP racers. Historically, Aprilia had always outsourced their engines; the rasping RS250 was powered by a two-stroke Suzuki RGV motor whilst the Pegaso

middle-weight trail bike benefited from an Austrian Rotax engine as used in the BMW F650. The Mille was the first machine from the Italian factory to sport an Aprilia power plant – a cleverly designed dry sump 60° v-twin that was light, compact and extremely powerful. Add to this a swingarm so beautifully crafted that it would not look out of place in the Guggenheim Museum and you have a guaranteed winner.

But Aprilia had greater designs. They wanted to take their machine into the World Superbike Championship and for this something special was required – a homologation special – the RSV1000SP.

Engine gurus Cosworth were brought in to breathe their magic on the SP's motor – the resulting adjustments in bore and stroke combined with forged pistons, redesigned heads (featuring a single liquid-cooled spark plug and five axis combustion chamber) and twin titanium exhaust cans resulted in a power increase of

almost 20% over the standard bike. This was all strapped to a redesigned frame that, in addition to being 20% stiffer, offered adjustable swingarm pivot, steering offset and the option to move the motor itself ±5mm for optimum bike setup.

With full carbon bodywork, aluminium fuel tank and Öhlins front and rear suspension completing the package the RSV1000SP was a true race bike straight out of the crate; so much so that it could not be sold as road legal in the United States. For those that could afford the €30,000 price tag, exclusivity was guaranteed as only 150 examples were produced worldwide – the minimum number required for World Superbike homologation.

SPECIFICATION

Capacity: 995.8cc
Type: V2 Cylinder – 8 Valve
Bore: 100mm
Stroke: 63.4mm
Compression Ratio: 11.5:1
Dry Weight: 185kg
Maximum Power: 145bhp @ 11,000rpm
Maximum Torque: 112.78Nm @ 8,500rpm
Maximum Speed: 170.9mph

Aprilia RSV-R Nera
2004 Italy

WITH FUTURISTIC, AGGRESSIVE styling more akin to an F117 Stealth Fighter than a motorcycle, the Aprilia RSV-R Nera is a machine that will turn heads whether blasting along the autostrada flat out at 160mph or just parked up outside the local café whilst

its owner enjoys a suitably strong espresso. Produced in a worldwide limited edition of just 200 individually numbered machines and described by its makers as "a motorcycle for the elite", this is about as exclusive and desirable an example of two-wheeled transport as you could hope to own.

Based on the hugely successful RSV-R Factory, the Nera is powered by a 997.62cc four-stroke longitudinal 60-° v-twin, carefully modified with the addition of friction-reducing molybdenum disulphide-coated pistons, a pair of lightweight magnesium head covers and beautifully CNC-machined intake couplings. All this, added to a pair of forged aluminium OZ wheels, full carbon fibre bodywork and tank and the ubiquitous selection of titanium nuts, bolts and fixings help produce a meaty 107Nm of torque and 141.4bhp at the crank whilst reducing dry weight over the standard model by an impressive 20kg to a positively svelte 175kg.

Attached to the gold-coloured trademark twin-spar frame sits a specially constructed lightweight swingarm, gleaming gold Öhlins suspension front

and rear and Brembo four-piston radial callipers with 320mm floating discs – all of which ensure pin-point cornering and formula one stopping power.

On the road the Nera is as impressive to ride as it is to look at. For such a physically large bike it is incredibly easy

to handle if you respect the stable of horses waiting to be let loose. Power delivery is smooth throughout the rev range with the long drive of the big-twin encouraging you to lay down the power early when exiting corners without fear of the back wheel spinning up and spitting you off.

Conceived as part of Aprilia's Dream Series, each Nera customer was bestowed with a collection of goodies just to remind them how special they are. Included in the substantial £25,000 (€35,000) price tag was an exclusive set of Dainese one-piece racing leathers, gloves and helmet, a miniature of your machine, a book, MotoGP hospitality with Aprilia Racing and a tour of the Noale factory. Now that's customer service for you!

SPECIFICATION

Capacity: 997.62cc
Type: V2 Cylinder - 8 valve
Bore: 97mm
Stroke: 67.5mm
Compression Ratio: 11.8:1
Dry Weight: 175kg
Maximum Power: 141.4bhp @ 10,000rpm
Maximum Torque: 106.9Nm @ 7,750rpm
Maximum Speed: 160mph

Benelli Tornado TRE1130
2007 Italy

BENELLI IS ANOTHER OF THE great marques of motorcycling history that in recent years has fought hard for its own survival. Founded in 1911 by Signora Teresa Benelli as a way of securing honest work for her six sons, the company reached prominence during the 1920s and 30s with a string of race wins including the Isle of Man TT. With a reputation for innovative technical design the Pesaro-based manufacturer wowed the motorcycle world in the 1970s with its Benelli Sei 750; a stunning in-line six cylinder with a sound like a V12 Ferrari at full chat.

Innovation returned to the factory in 2002 with the launch of its radical, naked TNT streetbike and the dynamic, sleek Tornado superbike both of which were designed by Coventry graduate and Terblanche protégé Adrian Morton. The Tornado was originally conceived as an 898cc triple for those desiring an exclusive track-orientated road bike; however, it soon received a version of the immensely powerful 1130cc motor that had made its debut driving the muscular TNT and with it, an increase in power from

an already astonishing 140bhp to a tyre-shredding 163bhp and 124Nm of torque. With a three-cylinder soundtrack more akin to a World War Two fighter plane, this happily propels machine and rider to a top speed of 175mph when conditions allow.

There is no doubt that this is yet another headturner in the grand Italian exotica fashion, but this is a machine that takes the principle a stage further. Huge ram-air intakes grace a front fairing that boasts three vertically stacked headlights whilst cooling of the under-seat mounted radiator is assisted by two electric fans that sit rear facing and visible below the diamond shaped tail light.

The machine's track-riding credentials are thoroughly borne out with the inclusion of an adjustable slipper clutch that prevents the rear wheel locking when changing down, a fully removable gearbox for rapid gear substitution, 50mm Marzocchi racing forks and the ubiquitous Brembo "Serie Oro" radial brake callipers. An uncompromising approach to construction for uncompromising high speed performance.

SPECIFICATION

Capacity: 1130cc
Type: In Line Triple
Bore: 88mm
Stroke: 62mm
Compression Ratio: 12.94:1
Weight: 195kg
Maximum Power: 163bhp @ 10,500rpm
Maximum Torque: 124Nm @ 8,000rpm
Maximum Speed: 175mph

Benelli TNT1130 Titanium
2006 Italy

WHEN ANDREA MERLONI, PRESI-dent of Benelli, described the TNT (Tornado Naked Tre) as "the natural heir to the '70s Café Racer" he hit the nail right on the head as it combines twenty-first century streetfighter styling with the impressive long-stroke 1130cc triple designed for the Tornado. Three versions of the TNT are offered – the basic TRE, the tweaked Sport and the all-out Titanium complete with carbon bodywork, dry clutch, titanium exhaust and forged Marchesini wheels.

Powered by an impressive long-stroke version of the 1130cc triple designed for the exotic Tornado superbike, the TNT is 100% muscle; producing 135bhp and an enormous 118Nm of torque at just 6,750 rpm – almost twice that of the Honda CBR600RR. Clever electronics come into play to help tame any excess grunt by allowing the rider to select one of two ignition maps at the touch of a button. Set to "controlled power", 30bhp is trimmed from the back wheel enabling even the most inept and heavy handed of riders to negotiate potholed town centres, rain soaked roads and to prevent scaring the wits out of their unsuspecting pillion passenger. However, touch the illuminated button next to the dash and you enter the world of "free power" where the full stable of Italian horses is unleashed. Fuel consumption is hit dramatically but this added cost is perhaps offset by the saving in front tyre wear caused by the TNT's propensity to spend most of its time on one wheel when the throttle is wound open.

One aspect which the TNT uncompromising attention to c the most exotic of machines a subjected to compromise to th ure of the designer (do not e about asking Pierre Terblanche running light mounted on the the Ducati 999) but the Benell sign of this. The bespoke swir perfect extension of the fram three-into-one exhaust system

SPECIFICATION

Capacity: 1130cc

Type: IL3 Cylinder – 12 Valve

Bore: 88mm

Stroke: 62mm

Compression Ratio: 11.5:1

Weight: 199kg

Maximum Power: 135bhp @ 9,250rpm

Maximum Torque: 118Nm @ 6,750rpm

Maximum Speed: 150mph

fully sculpted. Even the clever offset-cam chain adjuster and adjustable footpegs show an extraordinary sense of oneness with the overall design.

In an age of carbon-copy motorcycles where, to many, one machine looks much like another, the Benelli TNT stands out like a shining beacon. Its harsh, angular look may not appeal to everybody's taste but there is no denying that it is truly one of a kind.

Bimota Tesi 1D
1991 Italy

THERE ARE MANY WORDS THAT have been used to describe the Bimota Tesi 1D; weird is one of them and perhaps the most appropriate. Ever since the first ever bike rolled off the production line at the turn of the twentieth century, motorcycle engineers have sought to make things different. Sometimes this was for the sake of progress, sometimes for the sake of just being different to everything else. The Tesi falls somewhere down the crack that separates the two.

During the early 1980s Pierluigi Marconi, a young engineering graduate straight out of university, was brought onto the design staff at Bimota on the strength of his university thesis, or tesi in Italian. Through his studies, Marconi had explored various alternatives to the traditional front fork arrangement found on almost all bikes. The outcome of his research was a new and pioneering design for a hub centre double-sided front swingarm that utilised a single front shock absorber and was steered by two pairs of hydraulically controlled push-pull rods. Armed with this technical innovation, Marconi and Bimota set about creating a viable hub-steering motorcycle; the result, the Tesi 1D, was premiered at the 1991 Milan show to universal acclaim.

Powered by a water-cooled 904cc, 4-valve v-twin from the Ducati 851 and wrapped in sleek, if ill-fitting, white and red

bodywork, the 1D produced a more than respectable 113bhp thanks to a bespoke long-stroke crankshaft and Bimota's tuning capabilities. Instrumentation was by way of an unreliable, hi-tech LCD console which by modern standards would look more appropriate adorning an exercise cycle in the local gym rather than an Italian superbike.

There is of course the old adage, "if it ain't broke, don't fix it", and here lay Bimota's problem. Despite positive reviews from the motorcycling press, buyers, especially wealthy buyers, remained heavily sceptical about the whole concept. Even a double win in the Pro-Twins category of the Daytona 200 failed to win over the public's confidence

and with good cause. The direct steering of the conventional setup had been replaced with a complex system of spherical joints and bearings that encouraged flex and affected handling. With poor sales the Tesi 1D was withdrawn in 1994.

However, the spirit of the 1D lives on. In 2004 Bimota announced a new and highly advanced hub-steer machine. As innovative as its older cousin, the Tesi 2D represents another leap forward in motorcycle technology but, as ever, its success will rely entirely on the enthusiasm of an ever cynical public.

SPECIFICATION

Capacity: 904cc
Type: Twin Cylinder V 90°
Bore: 92mm
Stroke: 68mm
Compression Ratio: 10.2:1
Weight: 188kg
Maximum Power: 113bhp @ 8,500rpm
Maximum Torque: 85Nm @ 8,000rpm
Maximum Speed: 135mph

Bimota SB8K Santamonica

2005 Italy

PERHAPS THE FIRST THING TO mention about the Bimota SB8K Santamonica is the fact that for the same price you could fill your garage with a Honda Fireblade, a Suzuki GSX-R1000 and an Aprilia RSV1000R and still have enough change for new leathers, helmet and boots. But that is missing the point; the SB8K is a million miles from being any of these. If nothing else the chance of rolling up next to another one at the traffic lights is rather minimal to say the least.

The SB8K debuted in 2000 to critical acclaim. Based upon the company's existing SB8R road bike, it was initially produced in sufficiently small numbers as a homologation special for the World Superbike Championship. Very little was expected of the small Factory team but a sensation was caused when, in the second race of the season, Australian star Anthony Gobert took the machine to victory at Philip Island in atrocious weather conditions ahead of reigning champion Carl Fogarty's Ducati 998.

Powered by an unmodified liquid-cooled 996cc Suzuki v-twin taken from the TL1000R, the SB8K uses an enlarged airbox and Bimota's own injection

system, cleverly using servo-mounted radial injectors to direct the fuel to the most efficient position in the intake duct, to produce 142.6bhp and a thumping 105Nm of torque, an increase of almost 20% over the Japanese original. All of this is suspended from a unique modular frame that combines an aluminium front section and a carbon fibre rear.

Racing success created an unprecedented demand for the SB8K but troubled waters lay ahead. A series of on-track technical difficulties cast a cloud over the project and then a promised high profile sponsor, a jeans manufacturer, failed to materialise. Production was suspended as the cash-strapped firm fell into bankruptcy.

Rescued from the grave by a new management team in 2003, Bimota has gone from strength to strength developing exciting cutting edge new models, like the Delirio and DB5 Mille, and resurrecting the iconic SB8K. The latest incarnation, the special edition SB8K Santamonica, brings the machine bang up to date with full Öhlins suspension, six-spoke gold OZ wheels and Brembo radial brakes with floating disks. This is uncompromising exotica at its best. At almost £28,000 it had better be!

SPECIFICATION

Capacity: 996cc
Type: V2 Cylinder – 8 Valve
Bore: 98mm
Stroke: 66mm
Compression Ratio: 11.3:1
Dry Weight: 175kg
Maximum Power: 142.6bhp @ 9,750rpm
Maximum Torque: 105.5Nm @ 8,750rpm
Maximum Speed: 165mph

Bimota DB5 Mille
2006 Italy

THE ONE THING THAT CAN BE said about Bimota is that they know how to create head-turning motorcycles. From the hub-steering Tesi, through the YB8 and on to the SB8K their machines have always promoted innovation, passion and individuality.

During the summer of 2003, as part of the company's rebirth following several years in financial administration, the new Bimota management team briefed Sergio Robbianno, whose diverse portfolio includes the iconic Cagiva Mito, graphic designs for the AGV Ti Tech helmet and Spidi race suits, to create a definitive motorcycle for the new millennium – "Una vera Bimota". After considerable development, the prototype Bimota DB5 Mille was introduced to the public and press at the 2004 Munich Intermot show. An instant success, it was proclaimed winner of the prestigious Motorcycle Design Association Award in the Supersport category – an honour previously bestowed on the Yamaha YZF-R1 and the Ducati 999 – and received the public vote as most beautiful bike of the show.

Described by designer Robbiano as a composite-trellis, the DB5 features a unique chassis combining a Ducati style chrome-molybdenum steel frame with CNC-machined billet aircraft-alloy plates coupled to a tubular swingarm, again featuring billet end plates, which mirror the same technology. The engineering of the swingarm is particularly innovative; with the heaviest part of the structure, the steel tubing, being

SPECIFICATION

Capacity: 992cc
Type: V2 Cylinder – 4 Valve
Bore: 94mm
Stroke: 71.5mm
Compression Ratio: 11.3:1
Weight: 156kg
Maximum Power: 92bhp @ 8,500rpm
Maximum Torque: 83.4Nm @ 5,500rpm
Maximum Speed: 135mph

located close to the pivot and the lighter, aluminium ends supporting the wheel, unsprung weight is kept to a minimum although maximum rigidity is retained.

The DB5 Mille has the sharp, angular looks of a full blown MotoGP bike with its narrow frontal section, 992cc air-cooled Ducati 1000DS motor, fully visible behind a slashed back fairing, and twin under-seat exhausts. Front and rear Öhlins suspension, forged OZ wheels, 4-piston Brembo radial callipers and 298mm floating discs complete the exotic package.

BMW K1
1989 Germany

BMW, A COMPANY WITH A REPU-tation for building safe, reliable touring machines with Teutonic efficiency caused an enormous stir when, in 1989, they launched their flagship (or should that be starship?) K1. Whereas up to this

point, all BMWs and in fact all BMW riders looked alike, this new offering from the Bavarian bike-meisters with its brashly painted infeasible bodywork broke the mould completely.

The specification of the machine was, however, hampered by new "voluntary" limits set by the German government that stated no machine should produce more that 100bhp. For BMW to abide by this limit, a different approach to per-formance enhancement was required – aerodynamics. The solution was found in the K1's all enveloping fairing that incorporated integral panniers and the highly unusual and iconic oversized front fender. Wrapped up beneath this enormous plastic cocoon was a restricted shaft-drive liquid-cooled 987cc inline four-cylinder motor from the K100RS sports-tourer, a machine that had found favour with police forces across the nation for its bomb-proof reliability and copious power.

The big K1's chassis was far more tra-ditional than its Buck Rogers exterior, consisting of a tubular steel space-frame that incorporated the motor as a load-

bearing component. Light alloy wheels, the rear being a hefty 18x4.5 inch rim, were suspended at the front by a set of Marzocchi forks with the rear making

SPECIFICATION

Capacity: 987cc

Type: IL 4 Cylinder – 16 Valve

Bore: 94mm

Stroke: 71.5mm

Compression Ratio: 11.0:1

Weight: 259kg

Maximum Power: 100bhp @ 8,000rpm

Maximum Torque: 83.4Nm @ 5,500rpm

Maximum Speed: 149mph

use of BMW's Paralever system specially designed for shaft driven machines. Despite weighing in at a substantial 259kg the resulting package performed impressively with a top speed of 149mph and acceleration to 62mph in just 3.9 seconds whilst still returning a tourist-like 62 miles per gallon.

Handling was typically BMW with clean power delivery, effortless cornering and super-smooth high-speed cruising ability – a perfect machine for a dash from Frankfurt to the Côte d'Azur via the Alps. BMW continued production of the K1 until 1993 by which time almost 7,000 units had been produced.

BMW K1200S
2006 Germany

FOR MANY YEARS, ANYBODY looking for a big cc sportsbike would have considered BMW to be way off their radar. Whilst the Japanese delighted the world with Honda's CBR1100XX Super Blackbird, Kawasaki's ZX-12R and Suzuki's Hayabusa, those looking towards the German marque were at best offered the K1200GT or the Gold Wingesque K1200LT; ideal machines for an extended European tour with full luggage and a pillion passenger but not the most inspiring option for attacking knee-down alpine passes.

Enter the BMW K1200, the result of five years' specialist development by Munich's two-wheeled gurus and as far from a "K" series bike as you could imagine. Built to compete on a level playing field with the best oriental offerings, it could even be said that the design, bristling with technological advancement, actually tilts the pitch in favour of the Germans.

First the power plant - a 1,157cc DOHC transverse inline four cylinder. Nothing particularly special here you might think, but the big Beemer's motor is somewhat radical in design. Mounted low in the frame, the cylinders are fitted with smaller heads, thanks to a unique cam system, and angled forward at 55 degrees, considerably lowering the bike's centre of gravity. This is technology more akin to the MotoGP paddock than the high street. With 160bhp and 130Nm of torque at the back wheel, this machine sits comfortably in Blackbird and 'Busa territory – a theory confirmed by its 167mph top speed and the ability to accelerate to 62mph in around 2.8 seconds.

BMW's innovation does not finish at

the engine with the aluminium bridge chassis supported by a unique suspension system. The rear incorporates a new, lighter, stronger, single-sided version of the company's patented Evo-Paralever shaft drive system. The front Duolever system, a developed version of BMW's existing Telelever, utilises a cast, double-sided fork that pivots up and down and along its axis. This is mounted to a central single-spring strut that entirely separates the suspension from the steering almost eliminating brake dive and bump steer inherent with traditional telescopic forks. As if all of this is not enough, the K1200S incorporates a new system – ESA or Electronic Suspension Adjustment – which allows the rider to alter suspension settings from pushbutton controls located on the bars. Three modes are offered depending on riding style and riding conditions: comfort, normal and sports.

In the K1200S, BMW have created an amazing machine capable of touring, cruising and scratching. The perfect all-rounder? Not quite, but it's very close.

SPECIFICATION

Capacity: 1157cc
Type: 16v IL4
Bore: 79mm
Stroke: 59mm
Compression Ratio: 13.0:1
Dry Weight: 227kg
Maximum Power: 167bhp @ 10,250rpm
Maximum Torque: 130Nm @ 8,250rpm
Maximum Speed: 175mph

Buell Firebolt XB-12R
2006 United States

ERIK BUELL BUILT HIS FIRST MOT-orcycle, the rotary-valved RW750 racer, in 1983 under the banner of "Pittsburgh Performance Products". Testing and refinement continued over the following year but plans for full blown production were cut short when, in 1985, the AMA announced a change in racing classes that rendered the machine competitively

redundant. Undeterred, Buell soon cre-ated a new machine that drew upon his experience with Harley-Davidson motor-cycles. This motorcycle, the XR1000, had the honour of becoming the first ever American-built sportsbike. Realising the potential benefits of entering the sports market, Harley-Davidson acquired a 49% share of the business in1993. The Buell

Motorcycle Company was born.

Buell quickly developed a reputation for producing powerful streetbikes. Over the years, their Lightning and Thunderbolt models all but defined a new class of machine. For some time, production muscle bikes held a reputation for immense acceleration and straight-line speed, however, their ability to corner was often likened to that of a barge or shopping trolley. The Buell is different. This is a machine that can out-drag the best sports-bikes from the lights but, with a low centre of gravity and ultra-short wheelbase, is capable of cornering with pin sharp precision and crazy lean angles.

The XB12R Firebolt, the company's latest creation, takes the process a stage further. Its 14.5 litre fuel capacity is held within its aluminium frame whilst oil for the dry-sump 1203cc v-twin engine is housed in the swingarm doing away with the need for a separate oil tank. Combined with a mass centralising exhaust system mounted underneath the engine like a GP bike, the centre of gravity is kept incredibly low with the wheelbase reduced to a scooter-like 1320mm. Even the wheels are extreme in their design – incorporating ultra-thin six-spoke ZTL wheels with front 375mm fully floating perimeter discs and six piston callipers.

SPECIFICATION

Capacity: 1203cc
Type: Twin Cylinder V 45°
Bore: 88.9mm
Stroke: 96.82mm
Compression Ratio: 10.0:1
Weight: 179kg
Maximum Power: 100bhp @ 6,600rpm
Maximum Torque: 110Nm @ 6,000rpm
Maximum Speed: 130mph

Dodge Tomahawk
2003 United States

YES, THIS IS A MOTORCYCLE AND yes, you can buy one – if you have $555,000 to spare.

Designed as a concept vehicle, the Dodge Tomahawk was first brought into the astonished gaze of the public when Chrysler CEO Wolfgang Bernhardt rode it onto the stage at the 2003 Detroit Auto Show. Such was the interest, Bernhardt suggested that hundreds of machines would be built but the reality was rather a modest nine, constructed as "rolling sculptures" and not for highway use (although this was probably more to do with protecting legal liability).

Everything about the Tomahawk is big. The specially made tyres are set on twenty-inch rims to which are fitted huge perimeter-mounted rotors. What appear to be headlights at the front of the bike are, in fact, 70mm throttle bodies. The engine, a liquid-cooled V10 cylinder 8,277cc that normally resides in the Dodge Viper sports car, produces a titanic 500bhp and 712Nm of torque – about 55Nm more than a Ferrari Enzo. An oil change would require almost eight litres of the Mobil1 synthetic whilst refilling the coolant would swallow up over ten litres of antifreeze.

Estimated performance is as big as the specification would suggest with acceleration to 62mph in the region of two-and-a-half seconds and a maximum speed approaching 400mph – always assuming you could hang on to the bars at such a pace.

What prompted the American manufacturer of trucks and cars to create such a leviathan? Trevor Creed, senior vice president of Chrysler explained "The Dodge brand philosophy always challenges us to take life by the horns. In the case of the Tomahawk, grabbing and holding on to anything for dear life is a necessity.

SPECIFICATION

Capacity: 8277cc

Type: 10-cylinder V90°

Bore: 102.4mm

Stroke: 100.6mm

Compression Ratio: 9.6:1

Weight: 680kg

Maximum Power: 500bhp @ 5,600rpm

Maximum Torque: 712Nm @ 4,200rpm

Maximum Speed: +300mph (estimated)

Tomahawk is a scintillating example of what creative minds can do when given the opportunity to run free." A design exercise maybe, but perhaps this crazy example of American excess has given us a sneak view into the future. After all, what would those pioneering motorcycle manufacturers of the early twentieth century have made of the Yamaha R1 or the Ducati 999?

Ducati 916SPS
1998 Italy

THERE CAN BE NO DOUBT THAT the Ducati 916 is a design classic and not just in motorcycling terms. In 1993, Massimo Tamburini's creation set a benchmark by which all other machines were measured and fourteen years on that benchmark still stands. Viewed from any angle it always appears perfect, with a curvy single-sided swingarm and high level exhausts tucked away under the pillion seat, its clean, sexy oh-so-

Italian lines continue to turn heads and make hearts beat faster. Little wonder that a good number of these machines reside in enthusiasts' living rooms as art and not in a dusty garage with tins of paint and the lawnmower.

The 916 is not just looks, mechanically it is a real gem. The trademark steel trellis frame utilises the 916cc water-cooled L-twin motor as a load-bearing member to reduce weight whilst the cast aluminium single-sided swingarm mounts directly to the back of the crankcases keep the bike's wheelbase to a nimble 1,410mm but allowing the rear wheel to be easily changed with the sprocket carrier still in place.

Hot on the heels of the original 916, the 916SPS (Sports Production Special) was launched in 1996 as a World Superbike Championship homologation model. With bore enlarged from 96mm to 98mm, the original 916cc water-cooled L-twin's engine capacity was increased to the now legendary

996cc. Further performance improvements were made through remapped fuelling, double injectors for each cylinder in preference to the original singles and a pair of carbon fibre Termignoni exhaust cans. The complete package increased power from 114bhp to 134bhp whilst torque was boosted from 86Nm to 93Nm.

The bespoke 43mm Showa forks from the original 916 were retained with the addition of an Öhlins steering damper, however, the rear Showa monoshock was replaced with a superior Öhlins model. As always, brak-

ing was provided by Brembo in the form of twin 320mm floating rotors and four-pot callipers to the front and a single 220mm rotor and twin piston calliper to the rear.

In 1998 Ducati replaced the 916 with the 996, ostensibly the same machine but with the benefit of a larger bore motor developed from the SPS. This in turn was uprated in 2002 with the introduction of the 998 which incorporated a more powerful motor using 104 x 58.8mm, shorter stroke motor. The 998 was retired from the Ducati range in 2004 with the 998FE (Final Edition) to be replaced by the controversially styled 999.

SPECIFICATION

Capacity: 996cc
Type: V2 Cylinder – 8 Valve
Bore: 98mm
Stroke: 66mm
Compression Ratio: 11.5:1
Weight: 190kg
Maximum Power: 123bhp @ 9,750rpm
Maximum Torque: 93Nm @ 7,750rpm
Maximum Speed: 155mph

Ducati MH900evoluzione
2001 Italy

WHEN DUCATI FIRST exhibited the MH900-evoluzione as a concept bike at the 1998 Intermot fair in Munich, the object had been to showcase the abilities of the newly created DUCATIDESIGN department. Their mission statement, "To build bikes that matter. Bikes that endure. Bikes that raise the pulse of enthusiasts everywhere", was completely fulfilled.

Designer Pierre Terblanche, whose more recent creations have included the 999, Sport Classic and Hypermotard, took inspiration from a single machine in the Ducati factory museum, the 900 Desmo ridden to victory in the 1978 Isle of Man Formula One TT by "MH" – Mike Hailwood.

The MH900e was the bike Terblanche had dreamed of building for the last fifteen years. Its retro-modern look, like nothing else on two wheels, oozed a certain indefinable quality that exists in the best of Italian design. This was a bike with echoes of espresso coffee, Raf Vallone and the Ferrari GTO.

So strong was the public's reaction to the design following Intermot, the decision was taken to take the bike from dream to reality. In doing this the MH900e would become another first in motorcycle history – the first machine to be exclusively sold via the internet. Customers were invited to place their orders on the Ducati website from midnight at the turn of the new millennium. Within twelve hours all 2000 individually numbered machines were sold at a worldwide price of € 15,000.

Some aspects of the original prototype failed to make the final design such as the rear-facing camera that did away with the need for wing mirrors and the natty indicators mounted in the under-seat exhausts, however, many inspired details remained: the beautifully sculpted mounting points for the low screen, the polished chrome detailing around the single headlamp and the finned dummy sump that echoed the bevel-drive machines of the Seventies.

Although the Evoluzione produced a modest 75bhp from its fuel injected 904cc air-cooled L-twin taken from the redesigned 900ssie, it was no slouch on the road and fully capable of an 11.9 second standing quarter mile and a top speed approaching 140mph. With light steering, strong mid-range drive and high-speed stability, handling was typically Ducati but with a 1970s feel that complemented the individual personality of this unusual machine.

SPECIFICATION

Capacity: 904cc
Type: Twin Cylinder V 90°
Bore: 92mm
Stroke: 68mm
Compression Ratio: 9.2:1
Weight: 186kg
Maximum Power: 75bhp @ 8,000rpm
Maximum Torque: 76Nm @ 6,500rpm
Maximum Speed: 140mph

Ducati 999R
2005 Italy

THE DUCATI 999 WAS INTRODUCED in 2002 as a direct replacement for the 998 which, although timeless in design, was approaching its tenth year of sale. It was a brave decision for the Bologna factory to make. Tamburini's classic had won countless awards and adulation and, not least, the hearts of the motorcycling public who saw it as something truly special. Pierre Terblanche's brief for this new machine was straightforward; keep it simple and sexy and bring the company into the twenty-first century.

From the outset the design courted controversy. Ducati purists, saddened by the demise of the Tamburini design, showed difficulty in coming to terms with the sharper, more angular look of the new machine – its narrow body, stacked lights and aerodynamic fins being at odds with the smooth graceful feminine lines of the 916. But they say proof of the pudding is in the eating and with a stronger engine, better handling and improved ergonomics there was no doubting that the 999 performed well.

The 999R was introduced in 2003 as a homologation model from the World Superbike Championship. Its success

on the track was immediate. Neil Hodgson, riding for Fila-Ducati Corse, scored thirteen wins on his way to the world title with team mate Ruben Xaus taking seven victories and second place.

In its current incarnation, the Ducati 999R boasts 150bhp and a massive 116Nm of torque from the 999cc Testastretta (narrow head) liquid-cooled L-twin. Weight is kept to a svelte 181kg thanks to the copious use of magnesium and titanium components and gorgeous deep-red lacquered carbon fibre bodywork. The original cast grey swingarm is replaced with a box-section aluminium replica of the one fitted to its racing cousin. Öhlins suspension, Marchesini wheels and radial Brembo brake callipers with semi-floating disks complete the package for each individually numbered machine that is a true race bike for the road.

Also available is the especially liveried Xerox 999R that replicates the colours of the Ducati Corse World Superbike team. Other special editions have been produced in FILA colours as well as those of the Airwaves British Superbike team and Parts Unlimited from the US based AMA series.

SPECIFICATION

Capacity: 999cc
Type: L-twin cylinder
Bore: 104mm
Stroke: 58.8mm
Compression Ratio: 12.5:1
Dry Weight: 181kg
Maximum Power: 150bhp @ 9,750rpm
Maximum Torque: 116.7Nm @ 8,000rpm
Maximum Speed: 161mph

Ducati 1098S
2007 Italy

TO QUOTE THE DUCATI MARKETING speak, the new 1098 superbike was "designed by the racetrack" – a statement convincing enough when uttered by the factory that, since 1990, has won fourteen manufacturer and twelve rider World Superbike titles and in more recent times has appointed Claudio Domenciali, the CEO of the company's Ducati Corse racing division, to oversee the development of new road-going models.

A very simple ethic was employed in

the creation of the new 1098 – ultimate performance was the unquestionable goal. If any aspect of the project was not deemed to improve either performance or handling then it was to be dismissed. The culmination of their efforts has resulted in the creation of the world's most powerful twin-cylinder motorcycle and the lightest and fastest production Ducati of all time.

Its beating heart is the new 1099cc liquid-cooled Testastratta Evoluzione twin-cylinder motor. With an over-square 104mm x 64.7mm bore and stroke, compact cylinder heads topped with ultra-lightweight magnesium covers and MotoGP-derived oval throttle bodies which alone increase power output by an impressive 5bhp, the Evoluzione produces more power and torque in its standard trim than was achieved by the tuned Testastretta fitted to the homologation special 999R. Harking back to the glorious 998, the back-box exhaust system of the 999 is abandoned in favour of twin under-seat 57mm silencers mounted beneath the high, poised tail section – for those that enjoy a little more growl with

their v-twin, a colossal 70mm Termignoni system is also available.

Echoes of the Tamburini design are seen once again in the reintroduction of the single-sided swingarm and side-by-side headlamps albeit housed within a far more aggressively-styled nosecone. Ducati tradition is upheld by the use of a trellis frame – an increase in tube diameter combined with a reduction in wall thickness has resulted in a stiffer, stronger frame but with a weight saving of 1.5kgs.

Whilst the standard 1098 employs effective Showa suspension units front and rear, owners of the "S" version are treated to a sexy Öhlins package although both machines reap the benefits of a set of hugely powerful Brembo M4-34 Monobloc callipers usually saved for the

rigours of World Superbike racing.

Perhaps the most innovative technological aspect of the 1098 is its digital instrumentation taken directly from the GP7 MotoGP bike and controlled entirely by handlebar-mounted switches. Incorporated within the system is a full data acquisition system capable of recording three and a half hours of throttle, brake, rpm, gear selection, temperature, speed and lap times on a simple USB compatible memory device that allows the rider to analyse their performance using the supplied PC compatible software.

After several years of uncertainty with the controversial 999 it looks as if Ducati are once again at the top of the superbike food chain – that is until the next great thing comes to take its place!

SPECIFICATION

Capacity: 1099cc

Type: L-twin cylinder – 8 valve

Bore: 104mm

Stroke: 64.7mm

Compression Ratio: 12.5:1

Weight: 173kg

Maximum Power: 160bhp @ 9,750rpm

Maximum Torque: 122Nm @ 8,000rpm

Maximum Speed: 175mph

Ducati Desmosedici 16RR
2007 Italy

FOR MANY YEARS DUCATI WERE absent from the world of Grand Prix racing. Since the early 1970s the blue-ribband 500cc class had been essentially for two-stroke machinery – an area of technology unfavoured by the relatively small Italian manufacturer – so instead their efforts had been placed with Formula1 TT and World Superbike and to great effect. There was, therefore, a great deal of excitement when in 2002 technical regulations were amended to include four-stroke machinery of up to 990cc and an announcement was made by the Bologna factory that once again Ducati would contest the World Championship.

With Italian ace Loris Capirossi and Australian ex-World Superbike champion Troy Bayliss at the controls, the team opened the 2003 season in style with a podium in the opening round of the championship and a win for Capirossi in Catalunya. The bike, the Desmosedici GP3, was an instant hit with the fans – the ear-bursting howl of its V4 engine and unique look setting it apart from the rest of the paddock. Then, in 2004, another surprise announcement was made by the factory that sent a roll of excitement through Ducatisti the world over. They would produce a fully

road-legal replica of the MotoGP machine – the Desmosedici RR.

After two years' development the almost finished machine was first shown to the public at the Mugello racetrack in June 2006 with the announcement that the first of 400 machines would be delivered in July 2007.

Powered by a liquid-cooled 989cc L-four fitted with quadruple 50mm throttle bodies and gear-driven overhead cams, its four cylinders fire in a "big bang" asymmetric twin-pulse configuration allowing the motor to behave like a conventional v-twin. Strength is maximised and weight kept to a minimum by the use of sand-cast aluminium

cylinder heads and crank cases, magnesium engine covers and titanium valves and connecting rods. Completing the power package is a titanium 4-2-1 exhaust system with a so-called vertical exit concealed within the tail unit. Power is estimated to be in excess of 200bhp at 13,500rpm with torque figures to match resulting in a Grand Prix-like top speed of around 200mph.

However, all this high technology and exclusivity comes at a price – €50,000 (£35,000) to be exact. Not that this is likely to deter the most committed of Ducati fans eager to own the ultimate road-going motorcycle. After all, it's not every day you get to pop to the shops on a full-blown GP replica!

SPECIFICATION

Capacity: 989cc
Type: L-4 cylinder 16 valve
Bore: N/A
Stroke: N/A
Compression Ratio: N/A
Weight: 175kg est
Maximum Power: 125bhp est
Maximum Torque: 70Nm est
Maximum Speed: 165mph est

Ghezzi & Brian Supertwin
2006 Italy

SOME BIKES MANAGE TO DISGUISE their credentials under layers of streamlined plastic bodywork, others with a silky smooth exhaust note or a touristic riding position. The quirky Ghezzi & Brian Supertwin achieves none of this. It's big, brash, brutish and guaranteed to turn people's heads, even if they are only looking to find out what is making the ground shake beneath their feet.

Ghezzi & Brian was formed in 1995 by two friends, Guiseppe Ghezzi and Bruno Saturno, who wanted to design and build a motorcycle to take racing in the Italian Super-Twins Championship. Their partnership was an instant success, so much so that by the end of 1996 the Championship title was theirs. In 1999, after 9 victories in 32 races, they decided to take things a stage further and produce their first road-going machine – one that would capture the spirit of their racing masterpiece. The result was the Supertwin 1100.

Retro-modern café-racer bodywork sits perched on top of a single steel

beam chassis which utilises the Supertwin's massive 1064cc Moto Guzzi two-cylinder motor as a stressed member. The engine may be old-school but it still manages a respectable 94bhp and 98Nm of torque that pulls like a steam train from just 3000rpm. This is, after all, the same engine that powered their original track machine to Championship glory.

Guiseppe and Bruno have taken an uncompromising approach to bike design. Owning a Ghezzi & Brian motorcycle is akin to owning a finely tailored Saville Row suit – at this price you would not use nylon when the best silks are available. They know that their customers expect a superior service using only the best components and in no area do they disappoint. Front suspension is courtesy of the exotic Paioli factory, the rear from Öhlins. The twin polished stainless steel exhausts are built to order by Tubi Style who manufacture directly for Maserati, Ferrari and Lamborghini. Wheels are forged aluminium from Marchesini with braking provided by massive twin 420mm perimeter discs and four piston callipers. This is luxury motorcycling at its best.

But why Ghezzi & Brian? In Saturno's racing days there were just too many Brunos in the paddock so he adopted the exotic Anglicised version of the name – Brian.

SPECIFICATION

Capacity: 1064cc
Type: twin cylinder
Bore: 104mm
Stroke: 58.8mm
Compression Ratio: 9.5:1
Weight: 194kg
Maximum Power: 94bhp @ 8,000rpm
Maximum Torque: 98Nm @ 6,250rpm
Maximum Speed: 161mph

Harley-Davidson VRSCDX Nightrod

2007 United States

HARLEY-DAVIDSON HAD FOR MANY years, produced oversized über-cruisers powered by capacious v-twin engines that were perfect for coasting along the arrow-straight highways of Arizona but not the kind of machinery with which the term high-performance would normally be associated.

That was a job left to H-D's bad-boy sporting alter ego Buell. Then in 2001 something strange happened as out of the doors of the Milwaukee plant thundered the VRSCA V-Rod.

Gone were the 1950s' overtones, the heavy fenders, wide tanks and the agricultural engineering. Gone was the twin-cam air-cooled 45 degree v-twin. Here was a true twenty-first century cruiser, all sweeping curves, stainless steel and aircraft aluminium, powered by a high-tech 1130cc liquid-cooled DOHC sporting four valves for each of its two 60-degree cylinders and electronic sequential port fuel injection. The V-Rod was a wolf in wolf's clothing.

From the same DNA as the gleaming

SPECIFICATION

Capacity: 1130cc
Type: V2 Cylinder – 8 Valve
Bore: 100mm
Stroke: 72mm
Compression Ratio: 11.3:1
Weight: 292kg
Maximum Power: 121bhp @ 8,400rpm
Maximum Torque: 108Nm @ 7,000rpm
Maximum Speed: 140mph

VRSCA comes the VRSCDX – the Night Rod Special. Welcome to the dark side. Black wheels, black frame, black machine-slotted wheels and black motor – only the brushed shotgun end cans and 49mm custom forks offer any reflection and only the orange pin-striping and tank decals offer any colour. There is no doubt that this machine looks as mean as they come with wrap around shades being an essential rider accessory.

And it's not all show and no go. With 121bhp on tap from the Revolution motor and 108Nm of torque the Night Rod is, without a doubt, very fast – the sensation of speed amplified by the laid-back seat, upright bars and forward controls. Wind open the throttle on this machine and you really do find yourself hanging on for grim death as the big twin pulls hard from 3000rpm all the way to its 9000rpm redline. The V-Rod is never going to corner like a Buell but it still handles extremely well for a big cc cruiser and always feels positive wherever and however you point it.

It may not appeal to Harley traditionalists but the VRSC is a huge leap forward for a company all too often accused of hiding in the past.

Harris Magnum 5
1995 United Kingdom

IT'S NOT JUST THE ITALIAN ENGI-neering wizards who are capable of taking a stock machine, weaving a magic spell and creating awesome, class destroying superbikes. Brothers Steve and Lester Harris have spent the last thirty-five years fettling motorcycles in their workshop in deepest Hertfordshire. The culmination of their efforts is the Magnum; nothing to do with the excessively moustached 1980s Hawaiian detective though.

Based upon the company's modified Kawasaki Z1000 endurance racer the Magnum 1 appeared in the late Seventies, selling in small numbers to an informed few. The Magnum 2 was introduced in 1981. Powered by the 16-valve four-cylinder 1075cc motor from the Suzuki GSX-1100, it sported bodywork styled by Target, the creators of Suzuki's futuristic Katana. Kawasaki's GPZ provided the basis for the Magnum 3 but it was Suzuki GSX power beating at the heart of the Magnum 4.

The Magnum 5 is the Harris brothers' most accomplished creation to date. Powered by the 893cc liquid-cooled 16-valve DOHC from Honda's CBR900RR Fireblade, it offered improved performance over the Japanese plastic racing missile thanks to improved tuning and the fitment of Harris's own four-into-one steel exhaust system. A Magnum 5 could typically be expected to produce as much as 135bhp, a 9% increase of the stock 'Blade. With the donor bike known well for its vicious tendencies, the Magnum offered a more stable and controlled package thanks to an innovative tubular steel trellis frame and the use of an Öhlins rear shock that was far superior to the stock Showa unit.

SPECIFICATION

Capacity: 996cc

Type: V2 Cylinder – 8 Valve

Bore: 98mm

Stroke: 66mm

Compression Ratio: 11.5:1

Weight: 190kg

Maximum Power: 123bhp @ 9,750rpm

Maximum Torque: 93Nm @ 7,750rpm

Maximum Speed: 155mph

Not only did the Magnum 5 produce the goods in terms of performance, it was also a stunning bike to look at. A slippery fairing with twin round headlamps and high level exhaust gives clues to the Harris brothers' endurance racing origins without hiding away the gloriously engineered ladder frame beneath. In a world of copy-cat bikes, the Harris will always stand out as being something a bit more special – an endurance racer for the road.

Honda CBX1000
1978 Japan

WHEN LAUNCHED IN 1978, THIS machine redefined the muscle bike. The Honda CBX1000 was gorgeous to look at, thunderous to listen to and blisteringly fast to ride.

The creation of Shoichiro Irimajiri, an engineer who had cut his teeth on the HRC GP bikes of the 1960s, the CBX was a technological and engineering masterpiece. Powered by a highly developed six-cylinder 24-valve 1047cc DOHC motor, it produced an enormous 105bhp and over 83Nm of torque making it the most powerful production motorcycle of its time. Despite the use of hollow camshafts, magnesium engine covers and aluminium bars to help keep weight down, it still tipped the scales at a beefy 272kgs.

An innovative steel tubular frame acted as a backbone from which the stunning big-six engine was suspended, its beauty unhindered by ugly downtubes or braces. This, combined with the dramatic chromed six-into-two exhaust system gave the CBX a pure but purposeful look.

For all its bulk and power, the CBX was a surprisingly easy motorcycle to ride. The two foot wide motor was positioned well forward and tilted at a 33-degree angle to assist in providing leg room for the rider. With its brilliantly designed chassis and low centre of gravity it handled remarkably well through the corners but it was in a straight line where it came into its own. Sounding like all hell had just broken loose, it would pull like a freight train

SPECIFICATION

Capacity: 1047cc

Type: IL 6 Cylinder – 24 Valve

Bore: 64.5mm

Stroke: 53.4mm

Compression Ratio: 9.3:1

Dry Weight: 272kg

Maximum Power: 105bhp @ 9,000rpm

Maximum Torque: 83.4Nm @ 6,500rpm

Maximum Speed: 135mph

from 6000 rpm all the way through to the 10,000rpm redline and on to its maximum speed of 135mph.

For all its high technology the bike was, however, not a commercial success costing far more that many equally competent, if less attractive, machines of the time. It is though testament to the build quality of this amazing machine that so many still exist today in the hands of enthusiastic collectors.

Honda VFR400R NC30
1989 Japan

THIS BIKE HOLDS A SPECIAL PLACE in the heart of many a rider. Pocket-rocket performance combined with sublime handling and gorgeous looks have always assured the mini-racer's popularity.

Introduced in 1989, the VFR400R was sold through Honda UK dealerships between 1991 and 1994 but, with an expensive premium price-tag of £5899 (more than a VFR750!) few machines were sold through official channels. However, plenty of machines made it onto British roads thanks to the efforts of the grey import market where machines

destined for other world markets are purchased and imported into the United Kingdom by unofficial dealers.

In traditional Honda fashion, the chassis is an aluminium twin-spar from which is suspended an amazingly compact and bomb-proof 399cc V4 with gear driven cams. Ridden hard the bijou racer would produce about 63bhp at 12,750rpm and 36Nm of torque which it was capable of holding without a fault all the way to its screaming 15,000rpm redline, allowing speeds of up to 125mph. With the exhaust exiting from the left side of the bike, the right is kept clear for a fantastic view and fast changes of the tangentially

SPECIFICATION

Capacity: 399cc

Type: V 4 Cylinder – 4 Valve

Bore: 55mm

Stroke: 42mm

Compression Ratio: 11.3:1

Weight: 175kg

Maximum Power: 63bhp @ 12,750rpm

Maximum Torque: 36Nm @ 9,700rpm

Maximum Speed: 125mph

spoked rear wheel thanks to the unusual single-sided swingarm.

As one would expect, the VFR400 is not a machine designed for long distance trips to the South of France. With its lightweight flickable steering, race-bred geometry and free-revving engine it is a bike designed to be pushed hard and is the perfect tool for blasting around twisty B-roads or for storming over the Mountain at Cadwell Park.

Honda NR750

1992 Japan

THERE ARE SOME MOTORCYCLES that take innovation on to a totally different plane. There are others that are desirable beyond belief. There are, of course, some which are complete and utter failures. Very few machines manage to be all three.

Released at the same time as the class-defining Fireblade, Honda's NR750 was a technological marvel. At a first glance nothing may stand out as particularly unusual but closer scrutiny reveals that demonic things exist within its NR500-inspired 747.7cc V4 engine. Each specially designed oval-shaped piston, supported by twin titanium conrods, was capable of lifting eight valves. The resulting 32-valve motor offered similar

power characteristics to a V8. With gear-driven double overhead cams, Nikasil silicon carbide-lined cylinders, PGM-FI fuel injection and magnesium casings to reduce weight, this was the motorcycling equivalent of the space shuttle.

Despite reports of the time suggesting that pre-production test mules had produced a phenomenal 160bhp, Honda took the incredible decision to electronically limit power output to 125bhp at 14,000rpm. Although this gave the NR750 the distinction of being the world's most powerful 750cc production machine, the NR was no lightweight and any performance gain offered by the torquey, V4 was soon lost in compensating for its 222kgs of bulk.

With a conventional Honda twin-spar frame supporting a sexy single-sided swingarm, under-seat exhausts and Ferrari-inspired carbon composite bodywork costing more than most motorcycles, the NR750 is a gorgeous looking machine and a true design icon. At the time it had such an impact on other manufacturers that Ducati ordered a complete rework of their plans for the 916; comparing the two machines side by side can reveal many striking similarities.

But, all of this technology and innovation comes at a cost. And what a cost! When released in 1992 the NR750 was priced at £38,000 – the average UK house price was about £72,000. With only 200 machines ever produced of which a mere 15 were shipped to the United Kingdom it is very unlikely you will get to see one on the road today: most are safely tucked away in heated garages alongside the odd Ferrari or Maclaren.

SPECIFICATION

Capacity: 747.7cc
Type: V 4 Cylinder – 32 Valve
Bore: 101.2mm
Stroke: 50.6mm
Compression Ratio: 11.7:1
Dry Weight: 222.5kg
Maximum Power: 125bhp @ 14,000rpm
Maximum Torque: 68.5Nm @ 6,500rpm
Maximum Speed: 163.4mph

Honda CBR900RR Fireblade
1992 Japan

NEW MOTORCYCLES ARE FRE-quently described as being revolution-ary. Often they boast bizarre engine configurations, sometimes they are packed full of hi-tech electronics and once in a while they feature looks that just break the mould. But, more often than not, all these innovative bells and whistles are just a flash in the pan of biking history: the NR750's oval pistons,

the Bimota Tesi's hub steering. Real innovation comes from keeping things simple – something Honda achieved admirably in 1992.

At first glance there was nothing out of the ordinary about the CBR900RR Fireblade: a frame, bars, suspension, an engine, two wheels and a seat – all pretty straightforward. What was so unique was the fact that Honda's tech-nicians had built a 900cc superbike with 600cc supersport clothing. The 893cc 16-valve IL4 had similar dimen-sions to the motor fitted in the diminu-tive CBR600 but was capable of producing a blistering 124bhp in stan-dard trim. The trademark twin-spar chassis had been on a diet – the use of clever materials engineering had brought its weight down to less than that of the 600. This was a machine close to race-bike specification straight out of the crate, credentials heightened further by steering geometry never before seen on road-going machinery.

The resulting package was astounding and cornered like no other bike in its class. It seemed as if you only had to

look where you wanted to go and the light and nimble CBR would follow. For some the steering seemed so fast that many assumed it to be twitchy and unstable, however, this was far from the case thanks to superbly-matched suspension that always seemed capable of keeping the 160mph potential of the Fireblade well under control.

Testament to its stunning looks and unparalleled performance, the CBR900RR instantly became the United Kingdom's best selling motorcycle, overtaking the best that the other big Japanese three could offer and even outstripping the sales of Honda's own tried, tested and indestructible C90. Little wonder that the Honda Fireblade is considered a true icon of motorcycling history.

SPECIFICATION

Capacity: 893cc
Type: IL 4 Cylinder – 16 Valve
Bore: 70mm
Stroke: 58mm
Compression Ratio: 11.0:1
Dry Weight: 206kg
Maximum Power: 124bhp @ 10,500rpm
Maximum Torque: 89.5Nm @ 8,350rpm
Maximum Speed: 160mph

Honda RVF750F RC45
1994 Japan

THE RC30 IS DEAD. LONG LIVE the RC45!

Honda realised that, by 1994, their 748cc RC30 racer was beginning to look long in the tooth – outclassed by opposition from Yamaha and the new Ducati 916. For a company that had always thrived on its proud racing heritage this was bad news. Something special was required that could banish the opposition and put Honda back at the top of the superbike food-chain. Enter the RC45.

Powered by 749.2cc V4 equipped with PGM-FI fuel injection, the RC45 (also known as the RVF750F) promised race-bike performance and handling straight out of the crate to all those whose pockets sank deep enough to cover its astounding £17,980 price tag. For the American market the RC45 produced a paltry 97bhp thanks to the requirement of the DOT/EPA (Department of Transportation and Environmental Protection Agency) to fit a black-box limiter, however, unscrupulous use of a simple set of wire cutters would release another 10bhp. The European market faired slightly better having been offered 118bhp as standard but to release the RC45's full 150bhp potential an additional and costly HRC race kit was required.

Even as standard, the RVF was an impressive machine to ride. A sublime aluminum twin-spar frame with sharp race geometry married to a cast single-sided swingarm created a clean look, awesome handling and facilitated fast wheel changes on the race track. Showa's top specification 41mm USD forks and a rising rate rear monoshock formed a suspension package far superior to those fitted to other machines of the time. And then there is that motor. Despite lacking in pure horsepower compared to many of its contemporaries, the V4 was an engineering marvel. Sounding like an attacking World War Two dive bomber, the RC45 could blast away from the starting blocks like a guided missile not hitting its first-

SPECIFICATION

Capacity: 749.2cc

Type: V 4 Cylinder – 16 Valve

Bore: 72mm

Stroke: 46mm

Compression Ratio: 11.5:1

Weight: 189kg

Maximum Power: 119bhp @ 12,000rpm

Maximum Torque: 71.5Nm @ 10,000rpm

Maximum Speed: 168mph

gear redline until the clocks read 90mph.

Dogged by front end stability problems in its racing form, the RC45 was far from the all conquering hero that Honda had envisaged. However, following a single 1996 victory for Aaron Slight at Hockenheim, American rider John Kocinski proved the RVF's doubters wrong by taking the 1997 World Superbike Championship aboard the bike.

Honda CBR1100XX
Super Blackbird
2006 Japan

IT IS OFTEN AMUSING TO SEE HOW manufacturers classify their motorcycles. BMW's GS1100 is obviously an adventure bike, the Ducati 999 is obviously a superbike and Triumph's Rocket III is obviously a cruiser. Honda would have

you believe that the CBR1100XX Super Blackbird is a sports-tourer. The dictionary offers five basic definitions of "tour": pleasure trip, performing trip, playing trip, brief trip to see something, period of duty. All these might well describe an afternoon spent on the big Honda but the dictionary makes no mention of doing these things at 180mph.

The motivation for constructing a machine like this was pure and simple. Honda's title as manufacturer of the world's fastest motorcycle had been usurped by their arch rivals Kawasaki with the unveiling of their 175mph ZZ-R1100 in 1992. Now it was payback time.

With up to 164bhp and 119Nm of torque on tap from the mighty but conventional 1137cc liquid-cooled IL4 and a 10,800rpm redline, the Double-X is a veritable rocket-ship. Smooth power delivery belies the hyperspace-inducing acceleration that sets in as the needle hits the 5000rpm mark of the Super Blackbird; how appropriate to be named after the record breaking American SR-71 spy plane?

The ace card of this machine is its super-slippery bodywork. The CBR may not be the most radical or exciting of designs but many hours of development time have been spent in the wind-tunnel perfecting its arrow-sharp nose and low-profile curves. There are, however, no surprises with the chassis as once again Honda's highly rigid twin-spar aluminium frame takes centre stage.

Fast bikes need good brakes, in this case supplied by Honda's Dual-CBS (Combined Braking System) which operates both front and rear callipers regardless of whether the hand or foot-brake is used. Despite being a very effective way of bringing a bike back from

180mph and ideal in wet conditions, with panniers or with a pillion, to those riders more familiar with out-and-out sportsbikes the system can sometimes offer a lack of feel.

With the introduction of Suzuki's Hayabusa the Super Blackbird is no longer the fastest kid on the block but in the world of the super-tourer there are few finer ways of getting from A to B; just as long as there aren't too many corners en route!

SPECIFICATION

Capacity: 1137cc
Type: IL 4 Cylinder – 16 Valve
Bore: 79mm
Stroke: 58mm
Compression Ratio: 11.0:1
Weight: 223kg
Maximum Power: 164bhp @ 10,100rpm
Maximum Torque: 119Nm @ 7,250rpm
Maximum Speed: 175mph

Honda VTR1000 SP-2
2006 Japan

TOWARDS THE END OF THE 1990S Honda Racing Corporation was beginning to feel a little upset. For many years they had enjoyed countless victories as their RC30 racer controlled championships the world over. However, when it became outdated its replacement, the V4 powered RC35, failed to cut the mustard with only John Kocinski's astounding 1997 World Superbike championship title shining out in a

decade governed by the Desmodromic domination of the Ducati v-twins.

If you can't beat them, join them. In 2000, Honda launched the VTR1000 SP-1 (RC51) – their very own v-twin superbike – and completely upset the Ducati apple cart. The big twin, under the capable control of Texas Tornado Colin Edwards, stormed to victory in its debut race at the South African Kylami circuit before going on to win the 2000 World Superbike Championship title.

Unlike its RC35 predecessor, the road-going version of the RC51 was not offered as an exotic and expensive limited edition machine but as a full production model priced to compete with the best superbikes of the day. The Honda range already featured the similarly designated VTR 1000F Firestorm but there was little in common with the two machines – the SP-1 featuring fuel-injection instead of carburettors, gear-driven cams and a unique centrally positioned air intake duct that helped avoid the airflow turbulence generated by side mounted intakes.

With 136bhp on tap and capable of revving smoothly to 10,000 rpm, the

996cc liquid-cooled motor gave a satisfying crackle when powering the 200kg machine towards its 165mph top speed. With racetrack performance in mind, the twin-spar frame, 43mm USD forks and adjustable rear monoshock suffered on bumpy British B-roads. However, the SP-1 was designed as a race machine and it was on smooth roads and the track where it was guaranteed to excite.

In 2002 the SP-1 was updated and re-designated as the SP-2. With only the addition of new indicators and a 30mm higher screen, externally very little changed. There were, however, more significant changes to the motor as experience from the HRC works machines filtered rapidly to the road-going version. Twin 12-jet injectors, 62mm stacks and redesigned exhaust ports all helped towards a 4bhp increase in power whilst a lightened frame and exhaust system contributed towards a six kilo reduction in weight.

With changes in the rules allowing 1000cc 4-cylinder machines to compete in the World Superbike Championship, the SP-2 found its racing career cut short – replaced by the CBR1000RR Fireblade. It does, however, remain a popular machine for road-riding fans of v-twin motorcycles.

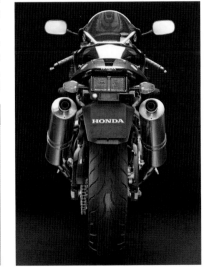

Honda CBR600RR

2007 Japan

WHEN HONDA FIRST LAUNCHED the CBR600 Hurricane in 1987 it was seen by many as a breakthrough in technology and design. One of the first fully-faired machines, it allowed Honda's designers to forego the need for frame and engine cosmetics in favour of pure engine development and power. With 80bhp on tap and a dry weight of just

182kgs it was easily the lightest and most potent super-sport machine available.

The CBR600F was introduced in 1990 but whilst it was visually a similar machine to its predecessor, engine improvements offered a 10bhp increase in power. The 1991 CBR600F2 featured a redesigned lighter frame, improved braking power and a leap in power output to an astounding 100bhp. Once again Honda's competitors found themselves playing a game of corporate catch-up. Further updates appeared with the F3 in 1995, the totally redesigned F4 in 1999 and the fuel-injected F4i in 2001.

2003 saw the introduction of a new machine to the class: the CBR600RR – Race Replica. Drawing straight from innovation and experience gained from Honda's RC211V MotoGP racer, the RR was a technological marvel. A compact IL4 utilised a centre-up exhaust and dual-stage fuel injection to produce 117bhp – a record for the 600cc class at that time – whilst 45mm cartridge forks and Pro-Link rear suspension coupled to a new aluminium frame helped optimise mass centralisation.

For 2007 Honda has once again put their successful CBR600RR through a complete wheels-up redesign that focuses on optimising the machine's power to weight ratio. At its heart is a new PGM-DSFI fuel injected 599cc IL4 so compact that, thanks to an innovative redesign of the engine's main shafts, it is actually smaller than an inline-4 250cc motor whilst still generating 118bhp and 66Nm of torque. Weighing in 8kg lighter than its predecessor, the new RR has shed 2kg from the engine and an astonishing 4.5kg from the die-cast aluminium twin-spa frame.

The resulting package is a fiery road-going super-sport race machine equally at home on the track or the twisty roads of an alpine pass. Power delivery is smooth but offers jet-propelled acceleration whilst the four-piston radially-mounted callipers and floating discs instil great confidence for late braking manoeuvres. The CBR600 has made many friends in its 20 years of service and the 2007 RR will be sure to carry the tradition forward.

SPECIFICATION

Capacity: 599cc
Type: IL 4 Cylinder – 16 Valve
Bore: 67mm
Stroke: 42.5mm
Compression Ratio: 12.2:1
Weight: 184kg
Maximum Power: 118bhp @ 13,500rpm
Maximum Torque: 66Nm @ 11,250rpm
Maximum Speed: 165mph

Honda CBR1000RR Fireblade

2007 Japan

WITH ITS SHARP, ANGULAR LOOKS, sublime handling and blistering performance, fifteen years on from the launch of the original Fireblade, Honda's 2007 model CBR1000RR demonstrates just how far bike technology developed in such a short period of time. This is, after all, the machine that propelled Ryuichi Kiyonari to his narrow victory over the Ducati of Leon Haslam in the 2006 British Superbike Championship.

Powered by a mass centralised 998cc liquid-cooled sixteen-valve inline-4 engine, the latest incarnation of this beast produces a whopping 170bhp (about the same as a Lotus Elise) and almost 115Nm of torque whilst weighing in at a scant 176kgs – an increase of almost 50bhp and 25Nm over the original with weight down by an enormous 19kg. A great deal of this extra power is thanks to the redesigned intake and exhaust ports which, combined with reduced combustion chambers create a higher compression ratio. Lighter engine internals combined with concentric intake valve springs and remapped fuel injection allow this free-breathing monster to rev to a 12,200rpm redline.

A great deal of this machine's finesse is to be found in the attention to detail lavished by Honda's exceptional engineers. It was relatively easy for them to shed bulk by the inclusion of a featherweight titanium under-seat exhaust system and narrower radiator but to improve braking power by increasing the front disk size by 10mm to 320mm whilst still managing to save 300g of weight by reducing their thickness by a mere 0.5mm is pure genius and beyond the thinking of many a manufacturer. Pinpoint handling accuracy is offered thanks to the highly developed MotoGP-inspired hollow-section cast aluminium twin-spar frame and gas-charged Pro-Link suspension integrated within the stylish but business-like rear swingarm.

This is twenty-first century motorcycle engineering at its absolute peak. The Blade lives on!

SPECIFICATION

Capacity: 998cc

Type: IL 4 Cylinder – 16 Valve

Bore: 75mm

Stroke: 56.5mm

Compression Ratio: 12.2:1

Weight: 176kg

Maximum Power: 170bhp @ 12,500rpm

Maximum Torque: 114.5Nm @ 10,000rpm

Maximum Speed: 178mph

Kawasaki Z1
1973 Japan

THIS TWO-WHEELED PIN-UP graced the shed door and bedroom wall of many a hairy biker in the 1970s and was the subject of numerous pub debates over the relative merits of a hot-panted girlfriend against excessive horse-power and two-wheeled freedom.

Known to many as The King, and with proportions and an appetite to match its Vegas-ensconced namesake, Kawasaki's 903cc air-cooled inline-4, was not just streets ahead of the opposi-

tion but already in another county. Whilst class-leading machines of the day – Suzuki's CB750, BMW's R90 and even MV's 750 Sport – produced in the region of 65 to 70bhp, the big Z1 churned out a class-killing 82 horses, supplying acceleration akin to a Phantom jet that would see many a nervous pillion gripping white-knuckled to the chromed cissy-bar en route to the top speed in excess of 130mph that allowed fellow riders to play a constant game of catch-up once the roads opened up and the throttle was twisted to the stop.

At 246kg it was undoubtedly a super-heavyweight but, nevertheless, handled remarkably well at low speeds. The same could not be said when belting along at

full rasp! When pushed it would seem as if the big motor was doing its best to break free of the steel twin-downtube frame forcing many owners to fit an array of non-standard dampers, shocks and springs in an attempt to calm the untamed beast. Remarkably, despite its bulk and performance, it was not until 1976 that the fitment of a second front disk and calliper became standard (although this was previously available as an optional extra), transforming the stopping power of the Zed immeasurably.

With its clean lines, wide bars and swept back exhausts, the Z1 still finds favour with many an enthusiast almost thirty-five years after it was launched to the public and it is true to say that it is still as good a looking machine as it ever was.

SPECIFICATION

Capacity: 903cc
Type: IL 4 Cylinder – 8 Valve
Bore: 66mm
Stroke: 66mm
Compression Ratio: 8.5:1
Weight: 246kg
Maximum Power: 82bhp @ 8,500rpm
Maximum Torque: 72Nm @ 7,000rpm
Maximum Speed: 132mph

Kawasaki GPZ900R
1984 Japan

WHEN KAWASAKI LAUNCHED their first liquid-cooled four cylinder motorcycle in 1984, the GPZ900R Ninja instantly became the must have bike of every wannabe racer and highway hooligan across the land.

With an enormous 113bhp on tap from its 908cc 16-valve inline-four which doubled as a stressed member for the lightweight narrow steel diamond frame, the GPZ maintained all the handling characteristics and compactness

of a 750cc race bike whilst being capable of showing a clean set of heels to all the fastest of the 1100cc competition such as Suzuki's Katana, Honda's CBR and Kawasaki's own iconic "Z". Power delivery was smooth and predictable but with a fantastic afterburner-like kick as the revs hit 8000 that made you hold on to the bars for dear life as the Japanese plastic racing missile blitzed from 0-100mph in under ten seconds on its way towards the 155mph top speed.

Weighing in at a hefty 228kg the GPZ was no lightweight, however, thanks to an innovative suspension system that incorporated anti-dive front forks and an air-assisted Uni-Track adjustable rear shock, it enjoyed astonishing handling for its day making the Kawasaki the bike of choice for fast road riders and production racers – it dominated the class at the 1985 Isle of Man TT. Later models were updated with wider rims allowing the fitment of fatter tyres and the original on-trend 16-inch front wheel was replaced with a more standard 17-inch unit.

Testament to its popularity, the Ninja remained in production in some markets until 2003. Undergoing few further updates or modifications during its life other than wider forks and larger front disks as other newer and faster machines arrived on the market, its status was downgraded from hi-tech superbike to budget priced fast-tourer.

SPECIFICATION

Capacity: 908cc
Type: IL 4 Cylinder – 16 Valve
Bore: 72.5mm
Stroke: 55mm
Compression Ratio: 11.0:1
Weight: 228kg
Maximum Power: 113bhp @ 9,500rpm
Maximum Torque: 85Nm @ 8,500rpm
Maximum Speed: 155mph

Kawasaki ZX-7RR Ninja
1996 Japan

WHEN IN 1995 THE BIG GREEN factory in Japan unleashed the successor to its highly successful ZXR750 many an eyebrow was raised. The all new Kawasaki ZX-7R with its enormous frame, seemingly built to withstand nuclear attack, wide fairing and air intakes the size of the Channel Tunnel, was a veritable behemoth of a machine, more akin to the construction methods of the company's heavy engineering division than the precision of the factory racing team. For all its heavyweight pretensions it did, however, have a number of things going for it.

First of all it looked fantastic – the big fat fairing, wide tank and chunky tail unit gave it the stance of a 100m sprinter ready to spring from the blocks in an Olympic final. Secondly, with over 126bhp on tap from a howling 748cc liquid-cooled inline-four it went like stink! And finally, they added horns and a forked tail to produce a leaner and more potent limited edition World Superbike homologation special – the ZX-7RR.

To the untrained eye there appears little visually to separate the standard model from the double-R but the obvious starting point is the mono seat unit and lack of pillion footpegs. Brakes were uprated from the standard Tokico system to exotic and expensive 6-piston Nissin callipers and 320mm disks whilst suspension came in the form of 43mm USD forks with 13-way adjustable preload and rebound and 17-way adjustable compression at the front and a 22-way adjustable Uni-Track monoshock at the rear. Less visible is the internal bracing of the frame, lightened subframe, replacement of the stock 38mm Keihin CV carburettors with quadruple 41mm flat-sided units and the fitment of a larger flywheel and a close-ratio racing gearbox.

All of this combined with a fully adjustable steering head angle and a swingarm mounted in an interchangeable eccentric plate allowing variation in the location of the pivot, the RR was veritably festooned with racetrack technology brought forward for public consumption on a fully road-legal machine that can still turn a head and see off a 600 ten years on.

SPECIFICATION

Capacity: 748cc
Type: IL 4 Cylinder – 16 Valve
Bore: 73mm
Stroke: 44.7mm
Compression Ratio: 11.5:1
Weight: 200kg
Maximum Power: 126.1bhp @ 11,199rpm
Maximum Torque: 84Nm @ 8,890rpm
Maximum Speed: 167mph

Kawasaki ZX-6R
2007 Japan

WHEN IN 2002 KAWASAKI launched their 636cc ZX-6R, in many respects they stole a march on the opposition. The old adage "there's no substitute for cubes" seemed appropriate at a time when motorcycle journalists and enthusiasts were obsessed with quoting figures as the be all and end all of bike comparison. After all, what easier way to trump the competition than to produce a more powerful machine simply by increasing capacity? We do not have to look very far back in the two-wheeled history books to see that for aeons the 500 had been the norm but, with the passing of time and the changing of trends the half-litre motors are now invariably found only in rather dull commuter bikes – the supersport category redefined by the advent of the nimble and racy 600s.

But, in launching this endeavour, Kawasaki had inadvertently set itself a whole new problem. In the all important sphere of Supersport racing, on the world stage the capacity limitation for four-cylinder machines remained at 600cc. To remain in the racing game they had no option but to continue to produce a bike that kept within the regulations – the 599cc ZX-6RR Ninja. This in itself was not a problem but it did mean that valuable resources were forced to be split between the ongoing development of both machines. In a financial climate where profitability is everything, something had to change, and for 2007 it did.

Gone was the 636: replaced instead with a new ultra-compact and high-revving 16-valve liquid-cooled 599cc, some 40mm shorter and narrower than

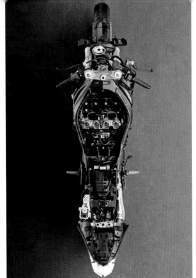

the previous motor that features across all ZX-6 models and is capable of producing 125bhp and 70Nm of torque. Race track influence extends to fully adjustable front and rear suspension, a close ratio cassette-type gearbox and the standard fitment of a slipper clutch to prevent the rear wheel locking up when changing rapidly down through the gearbox.

Beautifully sculpted with its catlike projector beam headlights, single air intake, satin black frame and high-pointing tail, the new machine is visually stunning and, as is the trend, heavily influenced by its MotoGP racing cousin – in this case the ZX-RRs of Randy de Puniet and Shinya Nakano. One thing is certain – it may be a huge leap forward for Kawasaki but it is still most definitely a Ninja!

SPECIFICATION

Capacity: 599cc
Type: IL 4 Cylinder – 16 Valve
Bore: 67mm
Stroke: 42.5mm
Compression Ratio: 13.9:1
Dry Weight: 164kg
Maximum Power: 134bhp @ 14,000rpm
Maximum Torque: 70.5Nm @ 11,500rpm
Maximum Speed: 167mph

Kawasaki ZX-10R
2006 Japan

THE ARRIVAL IN 2003 OF THE ZX-10R Ninja was a revelation. Like a phoenix from the flames, Kawasaki had, in a single stroke, returned from a wilderness of producing uninspired and lifeless two-wheeled anathemas to creating a class-leading superbike capable of taking on Yamaha's awesome R1 and the might of Suzuki's GSX-R1000.

Subtly refined for 2006 with a 4-2-1-2 underseat titanium exhaust system, revised geometry and new bodywork this is not a bike for the fainthearted, and if any glimmer of practicality appears on your list of must have attributes then look elsewhere. In essence this is an uncompromising track-orientated monster that just happens to feature lights, indicators and set of mirrors. In all other respects this is a highly tuned track missile just waiting to hurl you and your stomach through the right-to-left sweep of Donington's Craner Curves or launch you airborne over the crest of Cadwell Park's infamous Mountain.

Lurking under the sexy understated bodywork is a 16-valve 998cc inline-4. Pitched forward at 23 degrees and fitted with forged pistons, titanium valves, advanced twin-fuel injection and a mass centralising crankshaft mounted high in the engine casing, it produces a mind blowing 181bhp and a gargantuan 115Nm of torque – more than enough to help a brave rider see way past the wrong side of 180mph at the screaming 13,000rpm redline. Power delivery is, however, silky smooth throughout the rev range, never once threatening to pull your arms out of their sockets or pitch you skywards from the seat.

As well as being one of the fastest bikes you can ride the big ZX-10R is also one of the most satisfying. Forceful riding is well rewarded as the Kawasaki's twin-spar frame, extra-long aluminium swingarm and superb suspension soak up the bumps and ripples with ease instilling the rider with confidence by the bucket load. Big 300mm petal rotors (that's Kawasaki speak for wavy disks) are linked to super-powerful 4-piston Tokico radial callipers to provide unparalleled levels of stopping power with a slipper clutch, seemingly a de

SPECIFICATION

Capacity: 998cc

Type: IL 4 Cylinder – 16 Valve

Bore: 76mm

Stroke: 55mm

Compression Ratio: 12.7:1

Weight: 175kg

Maximum Power: 181bhp @ 11,700rpm

Maximum Torque: 115Nm @ 9,500rpm

Maximum Speed: 186mph

rigueur accessory on modern day sportsbikes, ensuring that everything stays happily inline when fast dropping down through the box.

The litre superbike market may be a crowded one with amazing machinery available from all the big manufacturers but, at about half the price of a Ducati 999R, if track-based excitement is what you desire you would be hard pushed to make a better choice than the ZX-10R.

Kawasaki ZZR1400
2006 Japan

SAVE YOURSELF SOME TIME. IF YOU are thinking about parting with about £9,000 to purchase Kawasaki's 218kg rocketship, just reach into your wallet, take out your driving license and cut it in half right now. It will save the bother of a nice young man in a blue uniform, fluorescent jacket and peaked cap doing it for you at a later date – and I'm not talking about a traffic warden upset about your parking on the double-yellows.

Ever since the Japanese manufacturer unleashed the mighty Z1 over thirty years ago, Kawasaki has enjoyed a mischievous reputation for producing all meat and no veg motorcycles capable of churning out massive horsepower and tractor-like torque. However, in more recent years its position as king of the high-velocity hill had been usurped by hyperspeed offerings from Honda and Suzuki in the form of the Super Blackbird and near legendary Hayabusa. Now it's payback time!

It looks like nothing else on the road. The ZZR1400's rounded front fairing is festooned with an array of no less than six lights not including the indicators, neatly fitted flush to the slippery bodywork. The front fender and even the mirror stems feature F1-inspired vortex-generating bumps to break up undesirable airflow patterns that could affect aerodynamics. You don't so much sit on this bike as sit in it.

Barely visible beneath all the wind-tunnel-developed plastic is the Kawasaki's 16-valve DOHC engine – all 1352cc of it – capable of producing a ram-air assisted 197.3bhp and an unbelievable 154Nm of torque. But this is no workshop-special drag bike in need of a rebuild after each high-speed outing. With thousands of fuelling variations controlled by a 32bit ECU, engine vibration reduced by a secondary engine balancer and the cam chain kept in check under the strain of vicious acceleration and deceleration by the use of a unique oil pressure-assisted tensioner, the ZZR is as reliable as it is powerful.

And what does all that power mean? The big-wigs at Kawasaki would tell you it means a lightning fast trip from 0-186mph with more than enough braking ability to take you safely back to zero thanks to the radial callipers and petal rotors. Impressive you might think? What they don't tell you is that the 186mph top speed is electronically limited to fall in line with a gentleman's agreement between manufacturers and that, with a little help from the tuning specialists, a double tonne is a reality. Now where's that license?

SPECIFICATION

Capacity: 1352cc
Type: IL 4 Cylinder – 16 Valve
Bore: 84mm
Stroke: 61mm
Compression Ratio: 12.0:1
Weight: 218kg
Maximum Power: 197.3bhp @ 9,500rpm
Maximum Torque: 154Nm @ 7,500rpm
Maximum Speed: 186mph

KTM RC8
2008 Austria

KTM, A MARQUE BEST KNOWN for indestructible off-roaders and radical super-motos, stunned the world when, just a month after launching their 990 Duke at the Milan show, they wheeled out their incredible RC8 prototype for the 2003 Tokyo show. It looked so right and it looked so KTM!

Since that debut, engineers at the Austrian factory have worked hard to make the dream a reality. Although originally specified with a 135bhp version of the 998cc 75-degree v-twin fitted to the 990 Duke, it is now expected to feature an all new 1150cc big-twin bringing it in line with new offerings from Ducati, Aprilia and Benelli. With development still taking place for an anticipated launch in the autumn of 2007, it is expected to produce in the region of 160bhp whilst generating a beefy 103Nm of torque at the back wheel.

Incorporating the motor as a stressed member to save weight, its frame is constructed of Chromalloy tubular steel to which is connected an enormous cast alloy double-sided swingarm. Radial Brembo brakes attach to titanium

nitride-coated USD forks from WP who also supply the rear mono-shock – unsurprising as WP are wholly owned by KTM Power Sports AG! With mass-centralisation the motorcycling watchword of the new millennium, the RC8's fuel tank is mounted beneath the rider's seat while the exhaust exits via a large belly pan-mounted silencer next to the swingarm in full MotoGP style adding to the uncluttered feel of the machine's sharp, angular-designed body panels.

SPECIFICATION

Capacity: 1150cc
Type: V 2 Cylinder – 8 Valve
Bore: n/a
Stroke: n/a
Compression Ratio: n/a
Weight: 1745kg
Maximum Power: 160bhp est.
Maximum Torque: 103Nm est.
Maximum Speed: 175mph est.

In announcing their intention to move from prototype to full production machine, KTM have undoubtedly rattled the cages of several manufacturers. Aprilia and Ducati will certainly be paying full attention to the efforts of their Austrian neighbour but, with new machines on the cards from both of these it is the Japanese who have the most to fear from this new batch of European metal. Perhaps the manufacturer's own words best sum up the RC8 and its potential impact on the motorcycling world. "She does not come in peace. She comes from KTM."

Laverda 750SFC
1972 Italy

THERE ARE MANY BIKES WHICH purport to call themselves "road going racers". In most cases the true similarities are somewhat vague with the actual race machine bearing little resemblance to the showroom model. The Laverda 750SFC is a true exception.

The Italian manufacturer first produced their 750S road bike in 1969 as a sports version of their already popular GT parallel twin. Launched in 1970, the 750SF (Super Freni) was fitted with an uprated front drum brake and internationally campaigned in endurance races finishing the season unbeaten. On the back of this enviable success, Massimo Laverda insisted that a racing special should be constructed – the Super Freni Competizione or SFC.

Painted bright orange so as to be easily seen during the all-night endurance events, the first batch of 20 race-spec machines were built during the spring of 1971 and fitted with high-compression pistons, 36mm Amal concentric carburettors, a close ratio gearbox and Ceriani 4LS brakes. Instrumentation was basic, consisting purely of a Smiths rev counter. Almost all of these machines were used as factory racers. A second batch of 75 machines, known as the 8000 series, was produced at the end of the year. Building from racing experience gained throughout the year, they were fitted

with a lighter fibreglass tank and longer exhaust down-pipes offering greater ground clearance.

With a reputation for reliability, exquisite handling and blistering performance, more and more SFCs started appearing on the road with the addition of an aftermarket speedometer and requisite number plate – having been designed for endurance racing, lights were already fitted as standard.

A third batch, the 11000 series, was further modified with the exhaust pipes now running directly underneath the motor. This not only served to improve the looks of the already stunning SFC but completely removed any issues of ground clearance when cornering. The most significant improvement in the design of the

Super Freni Competizione came with the introduction of the 16000 batch. Constructed in 1974, these machines were fitted with front and rear Brembo disk brakes, 38mm-Ceriani forks and a lightened crankshaft.

Known as the Electronica and launched a year later, the final edition 18000 series SFC was a state of the art piece of engineering fitted with Bosch electronic ignition and a modified primary chain cover. These last machines offered 70bhp and a top speed of 135mph.

Production of the 750SFC ended in 1976 with the introduction of the three-cylinder Jota but, even after thirty years, Laverda's "tangerine torpedo" looks as sporty as ever.

SPECIFICATION

Capacity: 744cc

Type: Parallel 2 Cylinder – 4 Valve

Bore: 80mm

Stroke: 74mm

Compression Ratio: 9.8:1

Weight: 206kg

Maximum Power: 75bhp @ 7,500rpm

Maximum Torque: n/a

Maximum Speed: 134mph

Martin Conquest 1200R
2007 United Kingdom

AFTER HIS ATHLETIC AND ADVEN-turous son was involved in a work accident and left wheelchair bound, designer Alan Martin decided to create him a vehicle that could live up to the outgoing and exciting lifestyle he had grown to love. He wanted to develop something that wasn't just about getting from A to B; he wanted a machine that would inspire its owner to plan trips from A all the way to Z!

If your impression of mobility transport for the disabled is limited to the idea of a Fiat Doblos with a raised roof trundling around the town centre then you need to think again. With its xenon front lighting cluster looking pure TVR and state-of-the-art LED brake lights, neatly mounted in the twin rear spoilers, that would easily grace the body of the most exotic Italian sports car, this, the all new Martin Conquest 1200, is seriously cool and an example of Motability gone mad!

If the front half of the Conquest looks familiar it is because it is taken straight from BMW's class leading R1200 cruiser, albeit with the forks raked further back to improve handling and stability. The reliable 1150cc air-cooled opposed twin drives both 17" alloy wheels via a prop-shaft and differential suspended from the highly engineered rear box-section aluminium frame. Aware that potential riders would be unable to make use of foot controls, gear changes are made by way of an F1-style button shift attached to the left-hand bar (a reverse gear is also fitted) whilst both front and rear brakes are linked and hand operated. For parking, a dash-mounted handbrake is used. As if the luxury of BMW power, TVR inspired bodywork and grand prix technology is not enough a high quality multi-speaker CD sound system is also fitted.

Entry to this unusual machine is by way of a remote-controlled ramp at the rear of the vehicle. Unlike so many other vehicles

SPECIFICATION

Capacity: 1150cc

Type: 2 Cylinder – 8 Valve

Bore: 101mm

Stroke: 70.5mm

Compression Ratio: 10.3:1

Weight: 600kg

Maximum Power: 83bhp @ 6,750rpm

Maximum Torque: 97.6Nm @ 5,250rpm

Maximum Speed: 100mph

for disabled users, the Conquest allows the rider to stay in their normal wheelchair whilst driving, with only a minor modification of the chair being required to allow it to safely lock into position.

As quick to sixty as an Audi TT and tested to well over 100mph, performance is unlikely to leave riders lagging behind their two-wheeled friends. And that is what the Martin Conquest is all about – freedom to be wild!

Mondial Piega Evo
2004 Italy

THE MONDIAL PIEGA EVO IS A machine that, on more than one occasion during its development, has come within a whisker of disappearing into obscurity as yet another motorcycling folly. Remember the antics of Lord Hesketh's V1000 and, more recently, Laverda's SFC1000?

Mondial, or F B Mondial to give it its full name – F B standing for Fratelli Boselli, was founded in Bologna in 1929 by the aristocratic Boselli family as a manufacturer of commercial vehicles. In 1948 and with the Italian nation still recovering from the ravages of the Second World War, Count Giuseppe Boselli met with the renowned motorcycle designer Alfonso Drusiani having decided he would like to produce a competitive 125cc race machine. Drusiani's machine was an instant success and within the space of a few short years the Mondial concern had taken ten World Championships in the 125cc and 250cc classes.

It was at this time that the embryonic Honda Corporation, having spent a decade producing simple, reliable and cheap motorcycles, was taking an interest in racing. Soichiro Honda's philosophy was simple – if you want to produce the best then speak to the best. In 1957 he approached the

all-conquering Mondial team for advice. Incredibly, especially considering the secretive nature of motor-sport in the new millennium, Mondial were delighted to assist even going to the extent of supplying the Japanese factory with a 125cc GP bike to examine. This generosity would pay dividends later in history.

After many years of corporate dormancy, Italian printing tycoon Roberto Ziletti purchased the rights to the Mondial name and set about building a machine to race in the World Superbike Championship. However, just two weeks prior to its launch at the Milan show, engine supplier Suzuki withdrew their support. Undeterred, Ziletti set about using his contacts within the Honda Racing Corporation and asked if he could borrow a v-twin from one of their SP-1 race bikes. Incredibly, Honda agreed and then offered to supply engine technology for both road and race machines.

The road-going version of the superbike racer, the Piega Evo, utilised revised mapping to increase power output to a healthy 138bhp from the 999cc liquid-cooled twin. This, combined with a 28kg weight saving over its Honda equivalent went towards producing a sharp, exotic race-replica in the best of Italian tradition capable of a speed camera-busting 165mph top speed. From the Öhlins suspension and radial Brembo brakes to the exquisitely sculpted bodywork manufactured by Carbon Dream, everything about the Piega oozes quality.

Mondial's troubles, however, did not end after the Suzuki debacle. Poor management at the factory caused production to suffer and, despite worldwide distribution and a full order book, the company descended first into chaos and then bankruptcy. The company was subsequently purchased by British-born but American-based automotive entrepreneur Andrew Wright but further legal proceedings have prevented additional machines from being produced.

SPECIFICATION

Capacity: 999cc
Type: V2 Cylinder – 8 valve
Bore: 100mm
Stroke: 63.6mm
Compression Ratio: 10.8:1
Weight: 178kg
Maximum Power: 140bhp @ 9,800rpm
Maximum Torque: 100Nm @ 8,000rpm
Maximum Speed: 165mph

MotoCzysz C1
2007 United States

MICHAEL CZYSZ HAS NEVER WON a World Championship. Nor has he ever apprenticed for the likes of Tamburini and Taglioni or worked for a motorcycle manufacturer. He is, though, a visionary, an innovator and very, very wealthy.

Czysz studied architecture at Portland State University before establishing his own firm, Architropolis, in 1990 and rapidly earning himself a reputation for the design of exclusive properties for individuals including Cindy Crawford and Lenny Kravitz, and trend conscious businesses like Roxie Records and E! Entertainment. He had always had an interest in motorcycles; his father had built a Norton that competed in the 1965 Daytona GP finishing second behind the factory MV Agusta of Mike Hailwood. Czysz had even spent some time as a racer campaigning 250cc Aprilias in the American amateur ranks.

MotoCzysz was formed with one clear intention: to build a bike capable of competing within MotoGP but not restricted by preconceived ideas about how a motorcycle should or should not be designed and engineered. The result is the MotoCzysz C1 990.

Everything about this machine demonstrates the lateral thinking and attention to precise detail for which Czysz is known. Each engineering problem has been approached with a fresh, uncluttered view. The incredibly narrow engine with twin contra-rotating cranks is a triple OHC Z-line 4. With the front two cylinders angled to the left and the rear two angled right, the gyroscopic forces inherent in traditional engine designs are all but negated producing a fast-handling machine with a neutral feel. The front suspension utilises a single spring mounted within the head tube whilst the aerodynamic machined fork-low-

ers offer a level of flex to counter the incredible stiffness of the C1's carbon fibre monocoque frame.

Czysz's plan for world domination

has, however, been met with a setback as Dorna Sport, organisers of the MotoGP World Championship, announced that the capacity limit for the premiere class in 2007 would be reduced to 800cc, instantly making the 990cc C1 ineligible for competition. Sights have now been set on the AMA championship although this in itself raises further problems regarding DOT/EPA approval. Nevertheless, this has not stopped MotoCzysz from pressing on with plans for the road-going model and a $10,000 deposit will secure you one of the first 50 machines due for delivery in 2007.

SPECIFICATION

Capacity: 990cc

Type: Z-Line 4 Cylinder – 4 Valve

Bore: 82mm

Stroke: 46.85mm

Compression Ratio: n/a

Weight: 170kg

Maximum Power: 200bhp @ 15,000rpm

Maximum Torque: 108Nm @ 15,000rpm

Maximum Speed: 200mph

Moto Guzzi MGS-01 Corsa
2006 Italy

A CREATION OF THE MOTO GUZZI Style Laboratory, the MGS-01 Corsa made its first appearance as a concept bike at the 2002 Intermot show to great acclaim. Guzzi had languished in obscurity for a number of years: branded as outdated and financially stretched it was only their acquisition by Aprilia in 2000 and the subsequent takeover by Piaggio that assured the survival of what was once Italy's largest motorcycle manufacturer.

Buoyed by the public reaction to the unusual design, company president Ivano Beggio announced that the concept would become a reality with the aim of producing the finished machine within two years. To achieve this, the project was handed to the design team at the exotic Ghezzi and Brian factory in Missaglia who had already reached fame with their wonderful Guzzi based Super-Twin (see page 40).

Using the motor from the v-twin Centauro as a base, a new race-bred engine was developed incorporating high compression Cosworth triple ring racing pistons, ceramic-coated cylinder walls and valves constructed from Nymonic alloy to increase resistance to high temperatures and extend wear; its

1,256ccs producing 128bhp and an impressive 110Nm of torque. With the MGS-01's wheelbase kept extremely short thanks to the integration of the gearbox

SPECIFICATION

Capacity: 1225cc

Type: V2 Cylinder – 8 Valve

Bore: 100mm

Stroke: 78mm

Compression Ratio: 11.6:1

Dry Weight: 192kg

Maximum Power: 128bhp @ 8,000rpm

Maximum Torque: 110Nm @ 6,200rpm

Maximum Speed: 155mph

into the timing case, Öhlins 43mm USD forks and adjustable monoshock and 505mm-long aluminium box-section swingarm, handling is optimised without compromising high speed stability.

Although the original project was divided into two parts - the first was to produce the limited edition non-homologated MGS-01 Corsa for track and racing use, the second to create the MGS-01 Serie as a full road-going type approved – the second phase was later abandoned making the MGS-01 unusual in the fact that it is fully available from high street Moto Guzzi dealers but is for track use only.

Moto Morini Corsaro 1200
2006 Italy

MOTO MORINI IS YET ANOTHER Italian marque that has seen new life breathed into it in recent years. From 1987, the brand had existed as no more than a piece of paper, first stating ownership by the Cagiva Group and then, in 1996, by Texas Pacific (who, inciden-

tally, also owned Ducati at the time). It was only in 2003 that new hope appeared in the form of three brothers – Gianni, Guido and Luigi Berti – who, having bought a controlling interest in the brand, employed the services of Franco Morini and designer Franco Lambertini. Within two years a new factory was built and a new range of motorcycles created. The first of these was the Corsaro 1200.

At its heart is the Bialbero CorsaCorta engine. Designed by Lambertini, this 1187cc 87 degree v-twin takes its name from the 250cc Morini Bialbero that captured three Italian Championships in the early 1960s and was dubbed "the fastest single cylinder in the world". The Corsaro is a true muscle bike producing 140bhp and an enormous 123Nm of torque at 6,500rpm compared to the 112bhp and 96Nm of the Aprilia Tuono and similar figures of Triumph's Speed Triple.

In Italian tradition, the tubular steel trellis frame utilises the motor as a stressed member to save weight and optimise flex and handling whilst the beautifully sculpted twin under-seat bi-conical silencers and tiny pillion seat give the bike a short, punchy look like a 100 metre sprinter in the blocks. The discrete rear indicators and LED tail light combined with a svelte cast aluminium swingarm offers a lesson to many a manufacturer about creating a tidy rear end. Meanwhile, to the front, wide and flat street-fighter bars guide beefy 50mm Marzocchi forks.

Early problems resulting in snatchy power delivery have now been ironed out by the Morini engineers and their Magneti Marelli ignition specialist counterparts – the difficulties arriving from a need to comply with Euro 3 regulations on emissions. The resulting machine is now smooth, fast and pulls like a tractor making the Corsaro 1200 the defining machine in its class with only the development of big-twins from the likes of Ducati and Aprilia threatening its position at the top of the muscle bike podium.

SPECIFICATION

Capacity: 1187cc
Type: V 2 Cylinder – 8 Valve
Bore: 107mm
Stroke: 66mm
Compression Ratio: 11.8:1
Weight: 198kg
Maximum Power: 140bhp @ 8,500rpm
Maximum Torque: 123Nm @ 6,500rpm
Maximum Speed: 156mph

MTT Y2K Superbike
2000 United States

LOUISIANA-BASED MARINE TURBINE Technologies will happily sell you many things: a powerboat, firefighting equipment or even a specialist craft for deploying US Navy SEALs into combat zones according to their brochure. They will also sell you a motorcycle. Some bikes are a work of true genius; other machines are insane. The MTT Y2K is both, and the only thing it is missing is an afterburner.

Powered by a Rolls Royce-Allison gas turbine engine more usually found in a helicopter, the Y2K generates a phenomenal 286bhp at an even more phenomenal 52,000rpm whilst producing a tractor-like 576Nm of torque – that is more than a Pagani Zonda sports car. But this is no one-off drag racer special. With $185,000 to spare you could own your very own road-legal jet-bike capable of 0-200mph in less than fifteen seconds and a top speed approaching 250mph. One Oregon-based MTT customer was even fined $10,000 for breaking a 45mph speed limit – at 233mph!

Everything about the Y2K is pure theatre. On turning the key the cockpit dash lights up orange, displaying essential oil and gas temperature figures – with an exhaust gas temperature of 1000 degrees Celsius this is one machine that you do not want to overheat whilst you are on board.

Another feature of the dash is an LCD TV screen attached to a rear facing bullet camera – mirrors become rather redundant on a machine capable of mach speeds like this. Pressing and holding the starter begins the turbine spinning then at 15% turbine speed jet fuel is injected and the motor crackles and bursts into life sounding uncannily like the Batmobile and smelling like a F16 fighter.

SPECIFICATION

Capacity: n/a

Type: Gas Turbine

Bore: n/a

Stroke: n/a

Compression Ratio: n/a

Weight: 227kg

Maximum Power: 286bhp @ 52,000rpm

Maximum Torque: 576Nm @ 18,000rpm

Maximum Speed: 250mph

With only two gears, selected from a handlebar-mounted toggle switch, great care is needed when changing down; a slipper clutch is an impossibility on a machine such as this and a premature down-shift at too high revs could result in, what the manufacturers euphemistically call, a catastrophic turbine failure. In short it would kill you!

In the land of Hummers and Cadillacs there is no shortage of customers for MTT's Y2K. Despite the astronomical cost and the 3,000 man hours of labour required to build each machine, the order books remain full.

MV Agusta 750 Sport

1973 Italy

DESPITE AN ILLUSTRIOUS HIS-TORY of building race-winning motor-cycles that netted the Cascina Costa factory a total of 37 World Championships between 1952 and 1973, Agusta had never taken the manufac-turing of road-going motorcycles seriously. After all Agusta's main operation was the construction of civil and military helicop-ters with the motorcycle-based Meccanica Verghera (MV) concern being little more than a hobby for founder Giovanni Agusta's autocratic race-mad son Domenico.

The arrival of the 750 Sport changed all of that. Based on the 500cc racer that had, over the course of eighteen years, taken six-teen World Championships in the premiere racing class, this new machine, resplen-dent in red, white and blue paintwork and chromed fenders, was stunning to look at, outstanding to ride and awesome to hear.

At its heart was a bored-out version of the 600cc four cylinder engine that had graced the company's uninspiring 600GT touring machine. In its reworked 743cc high-compression guise it sported quadruple Dell'Orto carbu-rettors, enlarged exhaust valves and a set of four sleek, chromed megaphone exhaust pipes resulting in an increase in power from a paltry 52bhp to a rippling 72bhp at 9,250rpm and a top speed approaching 136mph. Racing-derived details were apparent throughout from the gear-driven overhead camshafts to its sand-cast aluminium crankcases and the top-notch Ceriani forks and twin rear shock absorbers.

The only surprise element to the package was the continued use of the GT's shaft drive rather than the chain and sprockets of the factory racers; rumours persisted that this question-able design element was featured at the insistence of Count Domenico Agusta who feared that privateer racers could

take the 750 Sport to the track and, in doing so, take on the might of the factory race team. However, this failed to stop an enterprising few taking their machines to the workshops of Arturo Magni, the former head of the MV Agusta race team, who was happy to offer a very effective chain drive conversion to those who could afford it.

Testament to a fantastic design and dazzling looks the MV 750 Sport still looks fresh and relevant over thirty years on from the time it was first shown to the public. With retro-modern offerings now in vogue from the likes of Ducati with their SportClassic range and, of course, Triumph, could it now be time for MV to take a leaf out of their own history books and reinvent the Sport?

SPECIFICATION

Capacity: 743cc

Type: IL 4 Cylinder – 8 Valve

Bore: 65mm

Stroke: 56mm

Compression Ratio: 9.5:1

Weight: 230kg

Maximum Power: 72bhp @ 9,200rpm

Maximum Torque: n/a

Maximum Speed: 136mph

MV Agusta F4-CC
2007 Italy

SELL THE HOUSE, SELL THE CAR and sell the kids! Without any shadow of a doubt the MV Agusta F4-CC is the most stylish motorcycle available anywhere in the world, period, and whatever it takes you just have to find the € 100,000 to buy one!

For Italian designer Massimo Tamburini to follow his iconic creation, the Ducati 916, was never going to be an easy task as for many it was regarded as motorcycling perfection. Some people said it was a design that could never be

bettered. These people were wrong! With the launch of the 749cc MV Agusta F4-750, Tamburini turned a whole new page in creating a motorcycle that, just like its Ducati antecedent, was way ahead of its time. Many argued that it was, in fact, the design that should have graced the next generation of Ducati machines but sales of the 916 and its later derivative, the 996, were still strong and the Bologna factory was far from looking for a replacement. The sexy, sleek and oh-so very Italian F4-750 appeared to have it all but, as always seems to be the case when perfection is so close, it was flawed. No matter how aesthetically gorgeous this machine was it lacked a key ingredient. Oomph! Despite its 160mph top speed it quite simply could not match the performance of cheaper hi-tech Japanese rivals.

Then along came the F4-CC. Powered by an all new 996cc in-line four cylinder motor, the MV was turned into an Italian rocket-ship racer with 166bhp on tap –

an increase of some 30% over the standard F4-750 – and an astounding top speed of 180mph. There would be no further accusations of sluggish performance where this machine was concerned.

As has often been MV Agusta's way, the F4-CC has also been made available in limited edition "Special Production" form – first with the Agostini inspired AGO, then with the lightning-fast carbon fanatics dream machine – the Tamburini – and more recently with the super sexy Senna.

For 2007 MV Agusta has created the ultimate road machine: the F4-CC named after MV's president Claudio Castiglioni. Powered by a new 1079cc in-line four fitted with lightened rods, pistons and titanium valves and capable of producing 200bhp, the CC has an electronically limited top speed of 196mph – fast enough to just beat the heavyweight Hayabusa and ZZR1400 but without the excess lard that prevents the others from cornering like a sports bike should. With a new swingarm, uprated Brembo brakes and covered in a slippery carbon fibre body shell this is, without a doubt, the ultimate MV and possibly the ultimate road-going motorcycle.

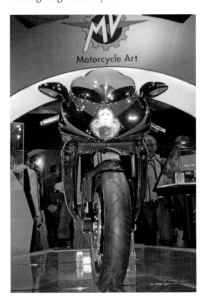

SPECIFICATION

Capacity: 1079cc
Type: IL 4 Cylinder – 16 Valve
Bore: 76mm
Stroke: 55mm
Compression Ratio: 13.0:1
Weight: 187kg
Maximum Power: 200bhp @ 11,750rpm
Maximum Torque: 113Nm @ 9,200rpm
Maximum Speed: 196mph

Petronas FP1

2005 Malaysia

WHAT DO YOU DO IF you're a motorcycling legend and have already set a lap record of the Isle of Man TT course, won fifty-nine superbike races, four World Championships and become a household name? Build your own bike and enter it into the World Superbike Championship, that's what!

With backing from Malaysian oil, gas and petrochemicals giant Petronas, former Ducati superstar Carl Fogarty formed Foggy Petronas Racing. The plan was simple – build a revolutionary racing motorcycle that could win the World Superbike Championship. However, things were not that straightforward. To qualify for the competition the FIM (Federation Internationale de Motorcyclisme) requires that 150 road-going machines are built and available for general sale. With the costs of research, development and manufacturing combined with the requirements of meeting countless type approvals, emission regulations and safety standards this would have been a considerable task

for an established motorcycle manufacturer but here was a bike racer from Lancashire prepared to take on the might of Japanese and Italian design. However, to the amazement of many who thought the task impossible, within a year the Foggy Petronas FP1 was taken from drawing board to reality – the first batch of 75 machines being produced in the United Kingdom.

With 80% of the newly developed race bike technology transferred to the homologation machine, the first road-going FP1 was launched with a public demonstration at the Galeri Petronas in Kuala Lumpur with no less than Carl Fogarty himself at the controls. The exciting new machine, the first to be developed from a race bike and looking like nothing else on sale wowed the crowds.

Powered by a Suter-developed 899.5cc reverse parallel triple, the road version of the FP1 produced 127.4bhp and 92Nm of torque – somewhat less than the 190bhp and 107Nm of the full-blown superbike but nevertheless sufficient to launch the would-be racer to a top speed of 165mph.

Sadly neither the road or race versions of the FP1 have been allowed to reach their full potential. After five years of trying, Foggy Petronas Racing closed its operations at the end of the 2006 World Superbike season. Despite achieving pole positions at Magny-Cours and Oschersleben, podium finishes were few and far between. The road bike, priced at a hefty £27,000 and only available directly from Petronas in Malaysia failed to grab the public attention, seeming just too unobtainable.

SPECIFICATION

Capacity: 899.5cc
Type: IL3 Cylinder – 12 valve
Bore: 88mm
Stroke: 49.3mm
Compression Ratio: 11.8:1
Weight: 181kg
Maximum Power: 127.4bhp @ 10,000rpm
Maximum Torque: 92Nm @ 9,700rpm
Maximum Speed: 165mph

Suzuki GS1000

1978 Japan

THERE WERE A COUPLE OF SIMPLE facts about Japanese muscle bikes of the 1970s that always seemed to ring true. First was that they invariably possessed a fantastic, reliable and powerful four cylinder motor capable of propelling a

grinning rider into the realms of silly speed riding. The second was that the said wonderful example of Far Eastern engineering would inevitably be suspended from a frame made either of Scottish girders or cheese thus offering the errant rider a machine with handling characteristics somewhere between a three-wheeled shopping trolley and a Grand Union barge.

With the arrival of the GS1000 the goalposts were well and truly moved forever.

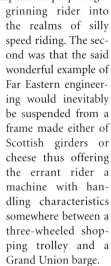

Here was a machine with greyhound-like performance from the blocks, that could outrun every other streetbike on the market but, crucially, was capable of matching the ride and handling characteristics of the best Italian, British and German machinery. Rock solid for high speed cruising and rail-like in its cornering, this was the first truly great big cc Japanese motorcycle; great enough to dethrone Kawasaki's iconic Z1000 from its top spot as most desirable road bike.

Its astonishing 997cc 8-valve DOHC motor actually weighed less than Suzuki's own GS750 motor thanks to the use of thinner crank cases, a lightened flywheel and the omission of the now outmoded and obsolete kickstart mechanism whilst still managing to produce an impressive 90bhp and 83Nm of torque. Its twin downtube steel frame was reinforced in several places to increase strength and rigidity and coupled to a beefed up tubular swingarm. Handling was further improved by the use of twin front disks, air-assisted forks and adjustable

rear shock absorbers.

For all its greatness the GS1000 was, however, flawed in one respect – it lacked soul and character. A rider of a 24-valve straight six Honda CBX would have his chrome-filled arrival heralded by a cacophony of rasping cylinders whilst a Moto Guzzi Le Mans pilot would ooze Italian style and charm. The GS was, without a doubt, boring to look at but that was not enough to dissuade bikers from parting with their hard earned cash who understood that this machine was a huge technological leap forward for the Far Eastern manufacturers. There may have been prettier bikes to choose from but none could compete with the complete, all round riding experience offered from the litre Suzuki.

SPECIFICATION

Capacity: 997cc
Type: IL 4 Cylinder – 8 Valve
Bore: 70mm
Stroke: 64.8mm
Compression Ratio: 9.2:1
Weight: 187kg
Maximum Power: 90bhp @ 8,200rpm
Maximum Torque: 83Nm @ 6,500rpm
Maximum Speed: 138mph

Suzuki GSX1100S Katana

1981 Japan

IN A TWENTY-FIRST CENTURY world packed with exciting, hi-tech designs like the KTM RC8, Bimota DB5 and MV F4-1000, Suzuki's twenty-five-year-old GSX1000S Katana can look a bit long in the tooth and rather under-stated but, when first launched in the opening years of the 1980s its sharp lines and aggressive nature were the ultimate in cutting-edge design – some-what appropriate for a motorcycle named after the razor-sharp weapon of a Japanese Samurai warrior.

Looking to make a clean break from the carbon-copy traditional output of the Far Eastern factories, Suzuki engaged the knowledge, experience and avant-garde stylings of the German-based Target Design Group. Their solu-tion was a million miles away from the sit-up-and-beg naked bikes that had gone before; the bars, racing style clip-ons, were swept low like an Italian fac-tory machine and the angular nose cone with its purposeful mini screen merged beautifully with the colour-coded tank and seat unit.

The Katana's motor was essentially the same trustworthy and reliable unit that had featured in the company's suc-cessful GSX1100, however, with the addition of a lighter camshaft and alter-nator, a redesigned airbox and carburet-tors and an all new exhaust system, power was increased over the standard machine by over 10% to 111bhp result-ing in blistering acceleration and a real-world top speed of about 140mph.

By sticking to their tried and tested twin downtube frame design, incorpo-rating fully adjustable anti-dive suspen-

sion and the fitment of twin 275mm rotors, the Katana handled exceptionally well for such a large and heavy motorcycle. Although the stiff suspension settings could feel a little harsh on the untrained rear if riding in the city, riders were offered confidence-inspiring braking and smooth, settled cornering on the open road.

Such was the big Suzuki's success; smaller engined derivatives based on the same futuristic styling were subsequently launched with 750, 400 and even 250cc machines being available in different world markets. Only after twelve years of sales was the Katana ultimately dropped from the manufacturer's range with the highly desirable GSX 1100SBE Katana Final Edition offered as the model's swan song.

SPECIFICATION

Capacity: 1075cc

Type: IL 4 Cylinder – 16 Valve

Bore: 72mm

Stroke: 66mm

Compression Ratio: 9.5:1

Weight: 247kg

Maximum Power: 111bhp @ 8,500rpm

Maximum Torque: 84Nm @ 4,000rpm

Maximum Speed: 140mph

Suzuki RG500 Gamma
1985 Japan

YET ANOTHER RACE REPLICA? Well, sort of! However, whereas so many of the so-called race-rep machines are little more than a blinged-up standard bike with a trick paint job, the RG500 was something a little more special – a full-blown street-legal replica of the Grand Prix motorcycle ridden to countless victories and multiple world championships at the hands of Barry Sheene, Franco Uncini and Marco Luccinelli. This was real-life racing technology offered at consumer level.

Weighing in at a svelte 166kg, the RG500 Gamma utilised an ultra-lightweight square-section cradle frame constructed from an aluminium/magnesium alloy from which the power plant – a water-cooled two-stroke 495cc square-four with rotary disc-valve induction, Mikuni flat-sided carburettors and power-valve-and-chamber exhausts that drew influence directly from Suzuki's GP workshops – was suspended. With about 95bhp available at the back wheel this equated to a power-to-weight ratio comparable to the best litre superbikes of the day.

But anybody who has owned or ridden an RG will tell you that it's not just about numbers – it's about the experience. With an arrow-straight power band from 2000 to 8000rpm the diminutive would-be racer accelerates with ballistic pace and precision to its 148mph top speed, always assuming you remembered to keep the 16.5" front wheel planted on the tarmac! Its sharp, race-inspired geometry, low front end and neutral wheelbase inspired jaw-dropping handling that seemed to straighten the tightest of chicanes whilst maintaining rock-steady stability through ultra-fast long sweeping corners.

The styling, whilst pure 1980s, still stands up well in a twenty-first century world – it's wrap-around fairing, tank and rear body panels resplendent in the blue and white of the Suzuki factory GP team. Perhaps the most prominent fea-

ture of the RG's styling was the exhaust system; tucked discreetly on each side behind the rider's footpeg was a tiny exhaust can whilst another pair was ele-

gantly concealed within the tail section – perfect to enable riders of lesser machines to identify exactly what has just passed them at warp speed.

Expensive and costly to maintain, the Gamma was only manufactured for four years but, fortunately, most fell into the hands of enthusiastic and knowledgeable owners and were well looked after. Such was its reputation, even twenty years on the RG commands a premium price on the second-hand market as there are few motorcycle aficionados who would not like to see one of these parked in their garage.

SPECIFICATION

Capacity: 495cc

Type: Sq 4 Cylinder – Rotary Valve 2 Stroke

Bore: 56mm

Stroke: 50.6mm

Compression Ratio: 7.0:1

Dry Weight: 166kg

Maximum Power: 95bhp @ 9,000rpm

Maximum Torque: 72Nm @ 9,000rpm

Maximum Speed: 148mph

Suzuki GSX1300R Hayabusa
2006 Japan

NAMED AFTER A JAPANESE BLACK-bird-eating falcon, Suzuki's Hayabusa is the original Japanese plastic racing missile. Laughably termed a "sports-tourer", much like its Honda Blackbird cousin (no, the joke isn't lost on them either), the über-fast GSX1300R is designed to ferry rider, pillion and luggage to the Côte d'Azur with the least possible fuss and in the shortest possible time one week, and

set land speed records the next.

When its futuristic form was released to the public in 1999 the 'Busa was touted as the first 200mph bike. However, in perfect conditions and on a very long stretch of road the naughty side of the double-tonne might well appear on the clocks (is there a non-naughty side at this kind of speed?) but the reality would be nearer to the 190mph mark. Hardly a slouch even

without the manufacturer's hype!

The key to the machines straight-line success lies first and foremost in its slippery skin. Developed through many hours of wind tunnel research, its jellymould form may lack the classic and graceful lines associated with the designs of Tamburini and Terblanche and might not win awards for aesthetic excellence but it does its job of cheating the wind impeccably. Even at hyper-touring speeds the rider remains untroubled hidden away behind the screen and fairing although, with its high pillion seat position, any two-up passenger has to remain well tucked in to avoid being blown away.

Aerodynamics are worth nothing without power and in the case of the Hayabusa this is delivered in bucket loads

courtesy of a liquid-cooled 16-valve 1298cc inline-four derived from that fitted to the GSX-R1100. Developing 175bhp and a gargantuan 138Nm of torque, superb mapping ensures instant power delivery throughout the rev range and a 0-60mph of less than three seconds and at 217kg it is light for its class.

In 2000 the 'Busa did undergo one small modification – the fitment of an electronic limiter that restricted top speed to 186mph – in response to the bureaucratic mutterings of Brussels who were less than impressed with the manufacturer's constant quest for speed. Bureaucracy has, however, failed to stop enthusiasts from achieving even greater speeds with a modified machine recording a 261mph pass on its way to an FIM world record for open-wheeled motorcycles.

SPECIFICATION

Capacity: 1298cc
Type: IL 4 Cylinder – 16 Valve
Bore: 81mm
Stroke: 63mm
Compression Ratio: 11.0:1
Dry Weight: 217kg
Maximum Power: 175bhp @ 9,800rpm
Maximum Torque: 138Nm @ 7,000rpm
Maximum Speed: 194mph

Suzuki GSX-R750 K6
2006 Japan

THEY SAY IT IS POSSIBLE TO HAVE too much of a good thing. This is just as true in the world of bikes as anywhere else; after all, for the average rider what use is a 1000cc engine and 175bhp? Of course, it makes for a blisteringly fast motorcycle but how much time is wasted nervously feathering the throttle out of corners rather than laying down the power by the truck load? This is where the GSX-R750 reigns supreme and why it is, quite possibly, the perfect all-round sports motorcycle.

It is still significantly more powerful than any 600cc machine on the market. Even the latest incarnation of the class-leading Honda CBR600RR trades close to 30bhp against the 750 Suzuki, not to mention 30% of the torque. And it is fast – at 168mph just a shade of the performance of a stock Ducati 999R. But with the GSX-R it's all delivered in a far more civilised, but no less exciting package. No brutal wheel-spinning power here, just smooth linear delivery that pulls like a freight train and never once makes you feel that someone or something else has taken charge of your life.

But the GSX-R's excellence is not just down to its powerful but civilised motor. Everything about this wonder-machine feels and looks just right. Its shape is ultra-modern but, without appearing garish or too radical, appeals to die-hard traditionalists and would-be MotoGP stars alike. The dash is big, bright and easy to read without becoming a distraction. The seat is comfortable and the controls always seem to be in the right places regardless of whether you are tall, short or happily somewhere in between.

Motorcycling perfection? Well, in a world where the goalposts are forever changing that's always going to be a matter for personal opinion and public debate but, in the mean time, if you're looking for the ultimate bike to whisk you to work Monday to Friday, take you to a track day on Saturday and out for a spin with your mates on Sunday morning, Suzuki's GSX-R750 is about as close as you're likely to get.

Suzuki GSX-R1000 K7

2007 Japan

THE ARRIVAL IN 2001 OF THE Suzuki GSX-R1000 sent out a bow wave so powerful that it threatened to drown the efforts of Yamaha, Kawasaki and Honda in one fell swoop. The big Gixxer's motor breathed 161bhp of pure fire (over 10bhp more than its R1 and Fireblade rivals), its handling was as sharp as a dagger and it could stop quicker than a fly hitting a windshield.

Not to sit on their laurels, Suzuki revamped the GSX-R in 2005 with yet more power and some slippery styling that was soon to be replicated on their smaller 600 and 750 models. But the Thou' was not just a success on the road. Under the capable hands of Australian star Troy Corser it broke the domination of the v-twins to become the first four-cylinder motorcycle to win the World Superbike Championship since Scott Russell's Kawasaki ZX-7RR had taken the title in 1993.

For 2007 Suzuki has done it once again, this time with a technological marvel that not only weighs less than its predecessor but actually produces more power whilst still managing to fall in line with the newly imposed and stringent Euro 3 emissions standards. The state of the art 16-valve 999cc liquid-cooled engine now features Suzuki's new SDTV digital fuel injection system which is said to revolutionise throttle feel whilst helping produce a colossal 178bhp. If this seems a little more power than you would care to handle – after all it is more than enough to reach a vision blurring 180mph – then help is at hand, literally! Fitted to the right handlebar is a three-way switch that allows the rider to select one of three engine power settings to match the road conditions and the volume of the pillion passenger's complaints. Completing the package is a fully adjustable suspension package and electronic steering damper, adjustable rearsets and 4-piston radial callipers with fully floating 310mm disks.

With such a comprehensive, powerful and efficient package the opposition is going to have to work very hard to once again take the high ground in the litre superbike battle.

SPECIFICATION

Capacity: 999cc
Type: IL 4 Cylinder – 16 Valve
Bore: 73.4mm
Stroke: 59mm
Compression Ratio: 12.5:1
Weight: 166kg
Maximum Power: 178hp @ 11,000rpm
Maximum Torque: 118Nm @ 9,000rpm
Maximum Speed: 180mph

Triumph Daytona 955i
2006 United Kingdom

THERE IS A STONE TABLET HIDDEN somewhere in the archives of the British motorcycle industry that decrees that all motorcycles built on these shores shall be inspired, exciting and full of muscle. Unfortunately this tablet remained so well hidden that from the end of the 1960s its hallowed text was all but forgotten. That is until a boffin at the Triumph factory stumbled across its words some time during the mid-Nineties and set to work designing the Daytona 955i.

The result was close to the traditional ideals of native bike building but didn't quite seem to hit the mark. Not that there was anything wrong with this particular bike – it's just that, save for a sexy single-sided swingarm, there really was nothing remarkable about it. Designed as a top-flight superbike it was no match for the likes of the new Yamaha R1 and could not hope to match the class killing power of the Fireblade. Instead it found itself regarded as a competent super-tourer judged alongside Honda's VFR and the Ducati ST2. That was until a radical redesign in 2002.

With reshaped ports and valves, a larger free-breathing airbox, higher compression and reworked ignition mapping, Triumph's folly had instantly surpassed all competition from BMW, Ducati and Aprilia to become Europe's most powerful production motorcycle with the 955cc 12-valve liquid-cooled triple's output increased by almost 15% to 147bhp. A further redesign in 2005 released an additional 2bhp with smoother power delivery throughout the rev range. Complete with its distinctive tubular aluminium frame and huge single exhaust can it conveyed a simple message to all - British muscle was back and it meant business!

Although not bred with the same racing pedigree as the best offerings from Italy and the Far East, the

SPECIFICATION

Capacity: 955cc

Type: IL 3 Cylinder – 12 Valve

Bore: 79mm

Stroke: 65mm

Compression Ratio: 12.0:1

Weight: 198kg

Maximum Power: 149bhp @ 10,700rpm

Maximum Torque: 100Nm @ 8,200rpm

Maximum Speed: 170mph

Daytona 955i is nevertheless a more than competent superbike capable of offering its rider an exciting and exhilarating experience whether on the open road or on the track. It does, however, manage to score points over the opposition by retaining the comfort and roomy nature of the 1997 original, making it the ideal mount for a high-speed two-up trip from Hinkley to St Tropez.

Triumph Daytona 675
2007 United Kingdom

HAVING JUST LAUNCHED A BRAND new motorcycle that has taken several years to develop, involved consumer focus groups, extensive testing and a major marketing campaign you would expect a manufacturer to feel rather pleased with itself and pretty buoyant about potential sales.

However, at the end of 1999 when Triumph launched its four-cylinder TT600 their feel-good moment seemed somewhat tempered by nagging doubts. The TT may have been a good bike but it

wasn't a great bike. The focus groups had demanded a 600cc four-cylinder machine over a triple or a twin, but was this purely because they were used to them and knew little of the other configurations? The slippery design was pleasing on the eye but rather lost against a sea of plastic-covered Far Eastern 600s. It was a decent enough machine but lacked the spirit and heritage of Britain's greatest motorcycle manufacturer.

Almost immediately Triumph set to designing a replacement. The first decision and the starting point for the entire project was the choice of engine configuration – a 12-valve triple. Then the geometry and ergonomics were sorted using a TT600-based test machine. The initial styling came not from an external agency but from within the company and the mind of a Triumph chassis engineer with no previous experience in bike design. All of a sudden the Hinckley-based manufacturer had a machine with style, spirit and, most importantly, identity. But would it perform?

The simple answer is yes! Hailed by many as the best ever British bike, the

Triumph 675 Daytona sports aggressive and exciting looks, sublime handling and blisteringly fast performance. Fed by a Keihin multipoint injection system with 44mm throttle bodies, its 675cc DOHC inline triple produces a whop- ping 123bhp and 72Nm of torque surpassing all other machines in the supersport 600 class and knocking on the door of the best 750 offerings from Japan. Cornering is a breeze thanks to a superb cast aluminium twin-spar frame and swingarm, complete with race-inspired adjustable pivot, which are married to 41mm Kayaba USD forks, and powerful radial Nissin callipers.

If you want to follow the countless hoards that yearn for faceless carbon-copy race replicas, then opt for something from Suzuki or Honda. If, however, a poised middleweight sports bike with race pretensions and an individual character is more your cup of tea you could do little better than opt for the 675 Daytona!

SPECIFICATION

Capacity: 675cc

Type: IL 3 Cylinder – 12 Valve

Bore: 74mm

Stroke: 52.3mm

Compression Ratio: 12.65:1

Dry Weight: 165kg

Maximum Power: 123bhp @ 12,500rpm

Maximum Torque: 72Nm @ 11,750rpm

Maximum Speed: 162mph

Yamaha RD500LC YPVS
1980 Japan

HAVING BUILT A REPUTATION IN the early 1980s by producing the powerful OW series two-stroke v-four 500cc factory grand prix bikes piloted by the likes of Kenny Roberts and Eddie Lawson, the imminent arrival in 1984 of Yamaha's race-inspired RD500LC was awaited with much excitement and expectation. Never before had just the mere thought of a new machine stirred such a level of anticipation and debate. This was one motorcycle that Yamaha could not afford to get wrong!

With its full fairing, tank and tail resplendent in a red and white Lawson-inspired livery the RD looked every inch a racer for the road. From its steel box-section frame was suspended a two-stroke liquid-cooled 499cc 50-degree v-four designed not around that from the company's OW76 racer but created by the melding together of two tried and tested RD250LC units – their bottom ends geared together to produce a single unit. With reworked induction, porting and the inclusion of Yamaha's patent YPVS power-valve system, the track-bred stroker churned out an impressive 90bhp and 67Nm of torque. As was typical for a two-stroke, performance was non-existent at low revs – the motor instead choosing to cough, splutter and smoke – but wind open the throttle past 6k and the lively half litre would crackle into life as if a demon had been awakened and catapult its rider on a ballistic to the 10,000rpm redline and 148mph top speed.

But the RD was not just about power and straight-line speed – it handled like the grand prix machine it aspired to be. With a superb chassis, light weight and powerful four pot callipers allied to 267mm rotors and outstanding ground clearance the Yamaha could corner and stop with precision and aplomb.

Despite its unquestionable heritage,

SPECIFICATION

Capacity: 499cc

Type: V 4 Cylinder – Reed Valve 2-Stroke

Bore: 56.4mm

Stroke: 50mm

Compression Ratio: 6.6:1

Weight: 173kg

Maximum Power: 90bhp @ 9,500rpm

Maximum Torque: 67Nm @ 8,500rpm

Maximum Speed: 148mph

and the fact that an RD could bring its owner closer to the experience of riding a grand prix bike as was possible without a contract as a factory rider, it failed to sell in significant numbers – a situation not helped by a high price and expensive running costs. Those who did take the plunge were treated to a truly unique riding experience and a little slice of contemporary motorcycling history.

Yamaha FZR1000 EXUP
1991 Japan

FORERUNNER TO THE NOW ICONIC YZF-R1, the FZR1000 EXUP was the must-have motorcycle of its generation. Oozing with, until then, infeasible levels of power and with silky smooth handling to match, Yamaha's big race replica is remembered well by all those who have been lucky enough to ride one.

The FZR's incredibly strong liquid-cooled 20-valve 1002cc inline-4 was a technological marvel. With its cylinders angled forward to improve fuelling via

the quadruple 38mm Mikuni carburettors and the use of the patented EXUP exhaust power valve system which adjusts the volume of the header pipe by use of an electronic servo-operated butterfly valve, an enormous and unheard of 145bhp was put at the disposal of the rider. Given the right conditions and a bit of determination this was a bike capable of a genuine 170mph and, with a standing quarter-mile time of a little over 10 seconds, the white-knuckle vertebra-crushing acceleration of a jet fighter launching from an aircraft carrier.

Perhaps this machine's most outstanding feature was its sublime chassis which married a superb reinforced aluminium twin-spar Deltabox frame to a set of taut 43mm USD forks and rear monoshock, adjustable for damping and compression, which had been engineered in conjunction with the Yamaha Motor Company's latest acquisition – the Swedish suspension specialist Öhlins. Weighing in at a little over 200kg, the resulting package ensured infallible straight-line stability whilst allowing the litre FZR to manoeuvre

through the twisties with the point and shoot accuracy of a 500cc GP bike.

Having produced such a remarkable

machine Yamaha could quite easily have expected to enjoy a reasonable period of longevity at the top of the sportsbike tree, however, another manufacturer had different ideas. With the launch of Honda's superlative Fireblade the goalposts had once again moved and were this time in danger of disappearing clean off the pitch. Yamaha fought back with the 1996 release of the YZF1000R Thunderace which utilised the FZR's motor but incorporated a new chassis and suspension package but it was not until the 1998 arrival of the YZF-R1 that the balance was truly redressed.

Yamaha V-Max 1200
1985 Japan

LOOKING MORE LIKE SOMETHING from a Judge Dredd comic than a production motorcycle, Yamaha's Pit Bull muscle bike was a revelation when it was debuted at Las Vegas in October 1984. Designed exclusively to appeal to the American market, the styling of the awesome V-Max drew its inspiration directly from big-block V8 muscle cars –

albeit without the associated cowboy boots and expansive top-lip facial hair – and was like nothing the biking world had ever seen.

Belying its humble origins as a power plant for the boxy XVZ1200 tourer, the 1198cc liquid-cooled 72-degree V4 motor underwent a complete transformation. The fitment of a healthy selection of top-shelf exotic tuning parts including lightened pistons, a racing crankshaft and high-lift cams was just the start as far as Messrs Ashihara, Araki and Kurachi – the V-Max design team – were concerned. They wanted yet more! The first thought was to install a turbocharger but, as these are invariably bulky, there was not enough space to accommodate one. Then they hit upon a breakthrough – V-boost. At low revs each of the motor's four Mikuni carburettors fed a single cylinder through an inlet tract. However, the tracts between the first and second cylinders and the third and fourth were separated by

servo-controlled butterfly valves which, as the revs increased past the 6000rpm mark, came into operation until, at 8000rpm, they were fully open thus allowing each cylinder to be fed by two carburettors on the intake stroke. This led to a massive increase in power from a modest 95bhp to a brutal 143bhp transmitted to the back wheel through a shaft final drive.

Sporting über-cruiser looks, dummy side-mounted alloy air intakes and upright riding position, the V-Max was never going to be the fastest machine on the block as far as top end speed was concerned although clinging on to this ferocious beast at 140mph was a challenge in its own right. Cornering? Forget about it! The big Yamaha came into its own on a standing start dash where, with the huge 150/90 V15 back tyre smoking like a train, a three-second 0-60mph was easily on the cards with the wrong side of a tonne appearing in a shade over six seconds.

This was, and always will be, the appeal of the V-Max. In a world where bikers debate the merits of suspension set-up, sticky rubber and lean angles there will always be a fondness for the sheer straight-line lunacy of a bike like this.

SPECIFICATION

Capacity: 1198cc
Type: V 4 Cylinder – 16 Valve
Bore: 76mm
Stroke: 66mm
Compression Ratio: 10.5:1
Weight: 262kg
Maximum Power: 143bhp @ 8,000rpm
Maximum Torque: 121Nm @ 6,000rpm
Maximum Speed: 140mph

Yamaha YZF-R7
1999 Japan

YAMAHA OFFERED NO SMOKE AND mirrors with their raison d'être for creating the might YZF-R7. It was simple – to win races. Such was their determination to ensure success on the track, even if you could afford the hefty £20,000 required to secure one of the 500 hand-built machines you would still have to prove that you had a season of top-level motorcycle racing planned out for the year ahead before the inscrutable Japanese factory would let you take one home.

Perhaps the most outstanding feature of the R7 was not the superlative engineering but the astoundingly clever way in which the Yamaha team had studied both the FIM regulations and the stringent international laws governing motorcycle emissions. Each of the 749cc motor's four plated cylinders was fed via triple titanium inlet valves from a huge 15-litre airbox and a state of the art twin-injector fuelling system. However Yamaha supplied the road-going machine with one of the twin injectors on each cylinder inactive thus limiting its power to a measly 105bhp but falling well within the environmental requirements of the bureaucratic environmentalist onlookers. Once in the hands of its owner the second bank of injectors could safely be switched and, with the addition of a free-flowing exhaust system and a modified ECU (permitted under the FIM's rules), an additional 30bhp would be unleashed. With a full-on race kit this could be expected to exceed 150bhp.

Use of vertically-stacked gear shafts, instead of a more commonly found horizontal arrangement, kept the R7's engine short allowing the fitment of a longer MotoGP-style swingarm with its pivot located closer to the centre of the bike, thus improving stability and weight distribution whilst still keeping the wheelbase ultra-short at just 1,400mm. Combined with a lightweight and

rigid twin-spar Deltabox II frame and a full Öhlins suspension package, the YZF-R7 handled with an unparalleled level of precision and accuracy

SPECIFICATION

Capacity: 749cc

Type: IL 4 Cylinder – 20 Valve

Bore: 72mm

Stroke: 46mm

Compression Ratio: 11.4:1

Dry Weight: 176kg

Maximum Power: 135bhp @ 11,000rpm

Maximum Torque: 72Nm @ 9,000rpm

Maximum Speed: 174mph

although, with track-based aspirations, the ride quality could be found a little harsh for illicit blasts on good old British B roads.

Production continued in strictly limited numbers until 2002 at which point the FIM regulations governing eligibility for the World Superbike Championship changed in favour of allowing an increase in capacity for four-cylinder machines from 750cc to 1000cc. Even with its P45 in hand, the R7 remains one of Yamaha's greatest achievements and will always be regarded as one of the most exciting production motorcycles ever built.

Yamaha YZF-R6
2006 Japan

EVER SINCE ITS LAUNCH IN 1999, the Yamaha YZF-R6 has led the way in the world of the road-going Supersport 600. Small, light, fast and exciting it was seen to have everything going for it. However, time allows others to catch up and, five years on, its position as class leader was under threat from superb offerings from Honda, Kawasaki and Suzuki.

Boasting sharp and more angular looks than before and sporting a short, MotoGP-style exhaust system, the introduction in 2006 of the new YZF-R6 saw the balance well and truly redressed. With a screaming redline of 17,500rpm, power from the all new short-stroke high-revving 20-valve 599cc inline-4 was up to 133bhp, an increase of some 13bhp over the original, thanks to an array of top-drawer components including secondary fuel injectors, lightened titanium valves, short-skirt pistons and a reworked crank. A totally new innovation was the introduction of a fly-by-wire throttle control. Developed directly from that used on Valentino Rossi's World Championship-winning YZR-M1 MotoGP bike, the system uses a cable-free system to offer improved fuelling control across the entire rev range.

The conventional aluminium twin-spar chassis combines both cast and pressed elements to create a balance between flex and rigidity and is coupled to a lengthened swingarm with its

pivot mounted close to the front sprocket. For the first time on a road machine a suspension package is incorporated that offers high and low speed compression damping adjustment for both the front forks and rear monoshock allowing for an even more

precise suspension set-up to be achieved. Braking is supplied by a set of 4-piston radial callipers allied to 310mm floating disks.

On the road, the R6 feels poised and ready for action – its high seat and low-swept bars instantly placing the rider in a racing crouch. Very tall riders might well find the machine's diminutive dimensions difficult to cope with but for most, with its raised footpegs encouraging you to move from side to side and hang off into every corner, it will suit just fine.

The 2006 YZF-R6 reset the bar in the supersport battle and it is now up to the competition to fight back. One thing is for certain, as riders we can only hope to benefit.

SPECIFICATION

Capacity: 599cc

Type: IL 4 Cylinder – 16 Valve

Bore: 67mm

Stroke: 42.5mm

Compression Ratio: 12.8:1

Dry Weight: 161kg

Maximum Power: 133bhp @ 14,500rpm

Maximum Torque: 68Nm @ 12,000rpm

Maximum Speed: 160mph

Yamaha YZF-R1 SP
2006 Japan

FOR MOST PEOPLE THE STANDARD model YZF-R1 would be machine enough to do any job required of it. With over 170bhp available with a casual twist of the wrist and looks sharp enough to upstage an A-list Hollywood superstar, Yamaha's flagship superbike has evolved immeasurably since its 1998 launch without losing any of the character and excitement of the original. But "most people" are not in the market for a very limited edition YZF-R1SP.

The rationale for the SP's existence is simple. Regulations for Superstock racing prevent the replacement or modification of many key components including suspension, wheels and brakes. What better way to give the R1 an instant advantage over others than to offer a machine with a higher specification straight from the crate? But this is more than just a case of taking a stock motorcycle, covering it in super-glue and ram-raiding Yamaha's racing stores in the hope that some of the parts will stick. The SP was developed from scratch, featuring specialist bespoke components designed, tested and produced solely for this project.

The R1's standard Deltabox twin-spar frame is reinforced, modified and lightened and the swingarm lengthened with an additional 16mm available between the pivot and axle. Shortened valve guides coupled with modified air intakes release an additional three horses, taking output from the SP's 998cc 20-valve inline-4 motor to a thundering 175bhp with the fitment of a slipper clutch as standard helping to keep everything in check whilst changing down hard through the box on the way into those tight corners and chicanes.

On most machines, the fitment of

silky-smooth progressive handling is taken without question but, having tested off-the-shelf equipment from the Swedish springmeister, Yamaha's engineers wanted to go one better. Influenced heavily by their experiences with the YZR-M1 MotoGP bike, they specified their own modified front and rear units which allow variable ride height and a wider range of adjustment giving the R1SP the most sophisticated and sorted suspension package ever seen on a production motorcycle from the Far East.

Öhlins front and rear suspension would be considered good enough for any job; its reputation for ultimate control and

To complete the package, a pair of beautiful forged-aluminium Marchesini wheels, painted gold to match the Öhlins forks and the body graphics, help shed another 400g of unsprung weight, an integral lap timer assists in recording your progress on the circuit (although it seems to require a degree in time and space physics to operate) and a smart plaque fixed to the upper triple clamp reminds you that you are, indeed, riding one of only 500 awesome YZF-R1SPs ever produced.

SPECIFICATION

Capacity: 998cc

Type: IL 4 Cylinder – 20 Valve

Bore: 77mm

Stroke: 53.6mm

Compression Ratio: 12.4:1

Dry Weight: 174kg

Maximum Power: 175bhp @ 12,500rpm

Maximum Torque: 106.6Nm @ 10,500rpm

Maximum Speed: 180mph

Available Now

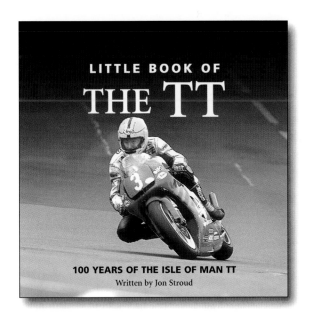

Available from all major stockists of books or online at:
www.greenumbrellashop.co.uk

The pictures in this book were provided courtesy of the following:

ROLAND BROWN WWW.MOTOBIKE.NET
JON STROUD
BMW UK
BENELLI
DAIMLER CHRYSLER
JOHN FALLON FOR LAVERDA IMAGES
FOGGY PETRONAS RACING
GHEZZI BRIAN
STEVE HARRIS FOR MAGNUM IMAGES
HONDA UK
KAWASAKI UK
MARINE TURBINE
H MITTERBAUER
MOTO CZYSZ
MOTOR MORINI
ROB BIRD FOR SUZUKI KATANA IMAGES
TRIUMPH MOTORCYCLES LIMITED
YAMAHA MOTOR CO UK
GETTY IMAGES
101 Bayham Street, London NW1 0AG

Book design and artwork by Newleaf Design

Published by Green Umbrella

Series Editors Jules Gammond & Vanessa Gardner

Picture Research by Ellie Charleston

Written by Jon Stroud